Green From Green III - Sustainable Harvest

- The Intersection of Agriculture and ESG

Jim Houlihan

Green From Green III - Sustainable Harvest
© Copyright 2024 by Jim Houlihan

ISBN 9798336175592 (Paperback)
ASIN: B0DD7PVXXK (eBook)

All rights reserved
The content contained within this book may not be reproduced, duplicated or transmitted without direct written permission from the author or the publisher.

Under no circumstances will any blame or legal responsibility be held against the publisher, or author, for any damages, reparation, or monetary loss due to the information contained within this book, either directly or indirectly.

Legal Notice
This book is copyright protected. It is only for personal use. You cannot amend, distribute, sell, use, quote or paraphrase any part, or the content within this book, without the consent of the author or publisher.

Disclaimer Notice
Please note the information contained within this document is for educational and entertainment purposes only. All efforts have been executed to present accurate, up-to-date, reliable, and complete information. No warranties of any kind are declared or implied. Readers acknowledge that the author is not engaged in rendering legal, financial, medical or professional advice. The content within this book has been derived from various sources. Please consult a licensed professional before attempting any techniques outlined in this book.

By reading this document, the reader agrees that under no circumstances is the author responsible for any direct or indirect losses incurred as a result of the use of the information contained within this document, including, but not limited to, errors, omissions, or inaccuracies.

Book design by Cover Designer
Jim Houlihan

Published by   **Skelligs Energy Solutions Limited**
                   V15 SC67, Ireland

https://skelligsenergy.com

DEDICATION

To those who remained, when the rest of us fled to the cities to work, or remain as digital nomads – homeless and rootless.

Unveil the future of agriculture with 'Green From Green III - Sustainable Harvest: The Intersection of Agriculture and ESG.'

This illuminating guide dives deep into the transformative journey of sustainable agriculture, from its historical evolution to its pivotal role in today's Environmental, Social, and Governance (ESG) landscape.

Discover lucrative investment opportunities and navigate the challenges of sustainable agriculture with insights from leading experts.

Explore groundbreaking innovations and technologies shaping the industry's future and gain strategic insights for policymakers and entrepreneurs.

Whether you are a policymaker, investor, entrepreneur, or part of the agricultural value chain, this book offers indispensable knowledge to drive greener solutions and secure a sustainable future.

Embark on this essential read and be at the forefront of the sustainable agriculture revolution.

CONTENTS

INTRODUCTION 1

1 THE EVOLUTION OF SUSTAINABLE AGRICULTURE 3

1.1 From Plows to Precision: A Historical Journey of Sustainable Agriculture 5
1.2 The Pillars of Sustainable Agriculture 8
1.3 Technological Innovations Driving Sustainability 13
1.4 Pioneering Paths: Case Studies - Sustainable Agricultural Practices 18

2 ENVIRONMENTAL, SOCIAL, AND GOVERNANCE (ESG) IN AGRICULTURE 24

2.1 The Pillars of ESG: A Framework for Sustainable Agriculture 26
2.2 Reducing Carbon Footprint and Conserving Biodiversity: A Dual Mandate for Sustainable Agriculture 30
2.3 Social Responsibility: Labour & Community Engagement 33
2.4 Governance: Transparent and Ethical Management in Agriculture 36

3 INVESTMENT OPPORTUNITIES AND CHALLENGES IN SUSTAINABLE AGRICULTURE 41

3.1 Identifying High-Potential Investment Areas within Sustainable Agriculture .43
3.2 Navigating the Terrain: Risk & Agricultural Investments 47
3.3 How Policy and Regulation Shapes Sustainable Agriculture 52
3.4 Success Stories of Investors in Sustainable Agriculture 56

4 INNOVATIONS AND TECHNOLOGIES SHAPING THE FUTURE 61

4.1　The Technological Renaissance: Precision Farming, IoT, and AI in Agriculture 63
4.2 Advancements in Aquaculture: Sustainable Practices for the Blue Economy .69
4.3 Renewable Energy for Agriculture & Aquaculture 74
4.4 Blockchain - Transparency & Traceability in the Food Supply Chain 79
4.5 Harnessing Innovation for a Sustainable Future 83

5 STRATEGIC ROADMAP FOR POLICY MAKERS AND ENTREPRENEURS 85

5.1 Crafting Policies for a Greener Tomorrow: Supporting Sustainable Agricultural Practices 87
By working together, we can build a more sustainable, resilient, and prosperous agricultural system for future generations. 91
5.2 Public-Private Partnerships: Collaborate for Sustainable Growth 92
5.3 Entrepreneurial Strategies for Entering the Sustainable Agriculture Market 96
5.4　Strategic Roadmap for Policy Makers and Entrepreneurs 100

ACKNOWLEDGMENTS

The author wishes to thank the various companies, brands and organizations for publishing the materials and success stories on the internet. These were broadly referred to in the various case studies used in adding colour to this book – without the success stories, it would be very hard to move the rest of the world in the right direction! *JH*

INTRODUCTION

In a small village nested between rolling hills and endless fields of green, a farmer named Elena faced a dilemma. Her family's land, cultivated for generations, was no longer yielding the bountiful harvests it once did. Soil degradation, unpredictable weather patterns, and market volatility all threatened their way of life to a greater or lesser extent...

One evening, as Elena sat on her porch, she contemplated the future of her farm and the legacy she would leave behind. It was then she stumbled upon the concept of sustainable agriculture, a beacon of hope that promised not just survival but thriving prosperity.

Welcome to 'Green From Green III - Sustainable Harvest: The Intersection of Agriculture and ESG.' This book is born from the urgent need to rethink how we produce our food, manage our resources, and invest in the future. The evolving landscape of sustainable agriculture is not just a 'nice to have' but a necessity for survival, deeply intertwined with Environmental, Social, and Governance (ESG) principles that drive today's global economy.

Our purpose is to provide a comprehensive guide that bridges the gap between traditional farming practices and modern sustainable solutions. We aim to empower policymakers, investors, entrepreneurs, and stakeholders in the agricultural value chain with some of the knowledge, insights and tools that might help foster sustainable growth for further generations.

Key themes explored in this book include the evolution of sustainable agriculture, the integration of ESG principles in agricultural practices, the investment landscape, and the innovations propelling the industry forward.

Each chapter delves into these themes, offering practical insights and strategic roadmaps for those looking to make a meaningful impact. The structure of the book is designed to take you on a journey:

- Chapter 1 examines the historical evolution of sustainable agriculture, setting the stage for current and future trends.

- Chapter 2 unpacks the role of ESG in shaping sustainable agricultural practices.

- Chapter 3 explores investment opportunities and the challenges inherent in this burgeoning field.

- Chapter 4 highlights cutting-edge innovations and technologies that are revolutionizing the industry.

- Chapter 5 provides a strategic roadmap for policymakers and entrepreneurs, offering actionable insights and recommendations.

The scope of this book is extensive yet focused, covering a wide range of topics without losing sight of the core principles of sustainability and ESG. However, it is not an exhaustive manual but a guide to inspire and inform, highlighting key areas of interest and importance.

The significance of this book lies in its contribution to the ongoing dialogue around sustainable agriculture. It offers a unique intersection of practical advice, strategic insights, and visionary thinking, all aimed at fostering a more sustainable and equitable future.

In summary, 'Green From Green III - Sustainable Harvest' is more than a book; it is a call to action. It invites you to join a movement that promises to transform agriculture, ensuring food security, environmental stewardship, and economic resilience for generations to come.

Like Elena, we all face a choice - continue on put current trajectory, or embrace sustainable practices that head off to a brighter, greener future...

1 THE EVOLUTION OF SUSTAINABLE AGRICULTURE

Source: Pexels

As the dawn breaks on a new era of agriculture, we find ourselves at a pivotal intersection where tradition meets innovation, and necessity drives transformation. The journey towards sustainable agriculture is not a recent phenomenon; it is a continuum that dates back to the earliest days of human civilization. This chapter embarks on a comprehensive exploration of this evolution, charting the course from rudimentary farming methods to the sophisticated, technology-driven practices that define modern sustainable agriculture.

In the beginning, agriculture was a simple endeavour, with our ancestors relying on basic tools and rudimentary techniques to cultivate the land and secure food for survival. These early methods, though primitive, laid the foundation for the agricultural practices that would follow. However, it wasn't long before the limitations of traditional farming became apparent, as growing populations and changing climates presented new challenges. The need for more efficient and sustainable ways to produce food became increasingly evident.

The transformation from traditional to sustainable agriculture has been marked by several key principles that have guided this evolution. At its core, sustainable agriculture seeks to balance the need for food production with the imperative to preserve natural resources and protect the environment. This balance is achieved through practices that enhance soil health, conserve water, reduce chemical inputs, and promote biodiversity. The principles of crop rotation, organic farming, and agroforestry have emerged as cornerstones of sustainable agriculture, each contributing to a more resilient and ecologically sound food production system.

Technological innovation has played a pivotal role in advancing sustainable agriculture. From the advent of mechanized farming equipment to the development of precision agriculture techniques, technology has continually pushed the boundaries of what is possible. Today, farmers have access to an array of tools and technologies that enable them to optimize resource use, minimize environmental impact, and increase productivity. Innovations such as drones for crop monitoring, soil sensors for precision irrigation, and, more controversially in some areas, genetically modified organisms (GMOs) designed for sustainability, are revolutionizing the way we approach agriculture.

The evolution of sustainable agriculture is best illustrated through case studies of successful practices implemented around the world. For instance, the adoption of no-till farming in the United States, and latterly in the EU, has significantly reduced soil erosion and improved soil health, while integrated pest management (IPM) techniques in India have minimized the reliance on chemical pesticides, resulting in healthier crops and ecosystems. In Africa, the implementation of agroecological practices has empowered smallholder farmers to improve yields and build resilience against climate change. These examples highlight the diverse and innovative approaches being taken to achieve sustainability in agriculture.

As we delve deeper into this chapter, we will uncover the historical context that has shaped sustainable agriculture, examine the fundamental principles that underpin it, and explore the technological advancements that continue to drive its evolution. Through a series of case studies, we will gain insights into the practical applications and successes of sustainable practices across different regions and contexts. By understanding the journey of sustainable agriculture, we can appreciate the progress made and recognize the potential for future advancements.

Join us as we embark on this exploration, setting the stage for a sustainable harvest that promises to nourish both people and the planet for generations into the future.

1.1 From Plows to Precision: A Historical Journey of Sustainable Agriculture

Agriculture, as the bedrock of human civilization, has undergone a transformative journey from rudimentary practices to sophisticated, sustainable systems. Understanding this evolution provides vital context for the contemporary push towards sustainability in agriculture, and reveals the pivotal milestones and innovations that have shaped our path.

The Dawn of Agriculture:

Early Practices and Innovations - The Neolithic Revolution
The origins of agriculture can be traced back to the Neolithic Revolution, approximately 10,000 years ago. This period marked humanity's transition from nomadic hunter-gatherer societies to settled agricultural communities. The domestication of plants and animals began, enabling humans to cultivate crops and rear livestock for sustenance. Early farming techniques were primitive, relying heavily on manual labor and simple tools such as digging sticks and rudimentary plows.

The Birth of Irrigation Systems
As agriculture spread, ancient civilizations like those in Mesopotamia, Egypt, and the Indus Valley developed early irrigation systems to manage water resources. These innovations allowed for the cultivation of crops in arid regions and supported the growth of stable, prosperous societies. The ability to control water supply marked a significant leap forward in agricultural productivity and sustainability.

The Agricultural Revolution - Mechanization and Increased Productivity

The Medieval Period: Crop Rotation and Soil Management
During the medieval period, European farmers began to practice crop rotation to maintain soil fertility and reduce the risk of crop failures. This method involved alternating different crops on the same land to prevent soil depletion. The introduction of the three-field system, which included fallow

periods, improved yields and contributed to the sustainability of agricultural practices.

The 18th Century - The Agricultural Revolution
The Agricultural Revolution of the 18th century brought about significant changes in farming practices in Europe and North America. Innovations such as the seed drill, invented by Jethro Tull, facilitated more efficient planting of crops, while the development of selective breeding improved livestock quality. Enclosure movements transformed common lands into more productive private farms, leading to increased agricultural output.
The Industrial Era - Mechanization and Chemical Inputs

The Introduction of Machinery
The Industrial Revolution in the 19th century introduced mechanization to agriculture on an unprecedented scale. Steam-powered tractors and threshing machines reduced the reliance on human and animal labour, exponentially increasing the efficiency and scale of farming operations. This period saw a dramatic shift from subsistence farming to commercial agriculture.

The Green Revolution - Chemical Fertilizers and Pesticides
The mid-20th century agriculture was further revolutionized by the Green Revolution, which introduced high-yield crop varieties, chemical fertilizers, and pesticides. The Green Revolution really refers to the development of high-yielding plant varieties – especially of wheat and rice, that increased food supplies in the 1940s-60s and staved off widespread starvation in developing countries. These advancements significantly boosted food production, helping to alleviate hunger in many parts of the world. However, the intensive use of chemicals also led to environmental degradation, soil depletion, and health concerns, highlighting the need for more sustainable practices.

The Rise of Sustainable Agriculture - A Response to Modern Challenges

The Environmental Movement
By the late 20th century, the environmental movement began to influence agricultural practices. Concerns over the negative impacts of industrial agriculture, such as soil erosion, water pollution, and loss of biodiversity, spurred interest in sustainable methods. Organic farming, which eschews synthetic chemicals in favour of natural inputs, gained popularity as a more environmentally friendly approach.

The Advent of Precision Agriculture
In the 21st century, precision agriculture emerged as a key component of

sustainable farming. This approach leverages technology such as GPS, sensors, and data analytics to optimize resource use and minimize waste. Precision agriculture enables farmers to apply water, fertilizers, and pesticides more precisely, reducing environmental impact while maintaining high productivity.

Key Innovations - Driving Sustainable Agriculture

Agroecology
Agroecology integrates ecological principles into agricultural systems, promoting biodiversity, soil health, and resilience. Practices such as polyculture, agroforestry, and cover cropping enhance ecosystem services and reduce reliance on external inputs. Agroecology represents a holistic approach to sustainability, emphasizing the interconnectedness of agricultural and natural systems.

Climate-Smart Agriculture
As climate change poses increasing risks to agriculture, climate-smart practices aim to enhance resilience and reduce greenhouse gas emissions. Techniques such as conservation tillage, crop diversification, and improved water management help farmers adapt to changing conditions while mitigating their environmental footprint.

The Intersection of Technology and Sustainability

Biotechnology and Genetic Engineering
Advancements in biotechnology have opened new avenues for sustainable agriculture. Genetically modified crops can exhibit traits such as drought tolerance, pest resistance, and enhanced nutritional content. While controversial, these innovations hold the potential for addressing global food security challenges sustainably.

Renewable Energy Integration
Integrating renewable energy sources such as solar, wind, and bioenergy into agricultural operations can reduce reliance on fossil fuels and decrease greenhouse gas emissions. Renewable energy technologies support sustainable farming by providing clean, affordable power for irrigation, machinery, and processing.

Policy and Governance - Facilitating Sustainable Practices

International Agreements and Frameworks
Global initiatives such as the United Nations' Sustainable Development Goals (SDGs) and the Paris Agreement on climate change have emphasized the importance of sustainable agriculture. These frameworks encourage countries to adopt policies that promote environmental stewardship, social equity, and economic viability in the agricultural sector.

National and Local Policies
At the national and local levels, governments play a crucial role in supporting sustainable agriculture through policies and incentives. Subsidies for organic farming, investments in agricultural research, and regulations on pesticide use are examples of measures that can drive the adoption of sustainable practices.

The Future of Sustainable Agriculture Innovation and Collaboration

The future of sustainable agriculture lies in continuous innovation and collaboration among stakeholders. Advances in technology, research, and policy will be essential to address the complex challenges facing the agricultural sector. Public-private partnerships, farmer cooperatives, and international cooperation will be critical in scaling sustainable practices globally.

Empowering Farmers and Communities
Empowering farmers and rural communities is fundamental to achieving sustainable agriculture. Providing access to education, resources, and markets enables farmers to adopt sustainable methods and improve their livelihoods. Supporting smallholder farmers, who often face the greatest challenges, is particularly important for fostering inclusive, resilient agricultural systems. In conclusion, the evolution of sustainable agriculture is a dynamic and ongoing process.

From the early days of simple tools and manual labour to the sophisticated technologies of today, agriculture has continually adapted to meet the needs of society. As we move forward, embracing sustainability in agriculture will be crucial for ensuring food security, protecting the environment, and promoting social equity. By learning from the past and innovating for the future, we can cultivate a more sustainable and prosperous world.

1.2 The Pillars of Sustainable Agriculture

Sustainable agriculture is built on a foundation of key principles that guide practices towards long-term agricultural productivity and environmental stewardship. These principles, often referred to as the pillars of sustainable agriculture, encompass a holistic approach that integrates ecological, economic, and social dimensions.

Understanding these pillars is essential for anyone involved in the agricultural sector, as they provide a roadmap for cultivating systems that are resilient, equitable, and capable of sustaining future generations.

Ecological Integrity

At the heart of sustainable agriculture lies the principle of ecological integrity. This principle emphasizes the importance of maintaining the health of ecosystems, which are the backbone of agricultural productivity. Ecological integrity involves practices that protect soil health, biodiversity, and water resources, ensuring that agricultural activities do not degrade the natural environment.

- Soil Health - Soil is a living, dynamic system that provides essential nutrients to plants. Sustainable agriculture practices aim to enhance soil health through methods such as crop rotation, cover cropping, and reduced tillage. These practices help maintain organic matter, improve soil structure, and promote beneficial microbial activity. Healthy soils are more resilient to erosion, retain water more effectively, and reduce the need for chemical inputs.
- Biodiversity - Biodiversity is crucial for creating resilient agricultural systems. Diverse ecosystems are better equipped to withstand pests, diseases, and climate variability. Sustainable agriculture promotes biodiversity through practices such as polycultures, agroforestry, and the conservation of natural habitats. By fostering a variety of species, these practices create a balanced ecosystem that supports pollinators, natural pest predators, and soil organisms.
- Water Management - Water is a precious resource in agriculture, and its sustainable use is vital for ensuring long-term productivity. Sustainable water management practices include efficient irrigation systems, rainwater harvesting, and the protection of water bodies from contamination. These practices help conserve water, reduce runoff and erosion, and maintain the quality of water resources.

Economic Viability

For sustainable agriculture to be truly sustainable, it must also be economically viable. This principle emphasizes the need for agricultural systems to be profitable, providing a stable income for farmers and other stakeholders.

Economic viability ensures that sustainable practices are not only environmentally friendly but also financially feasible.

- Market Access – Fair access to markets is a critical component of economic viability. Sustainable agriculture often involves the production of niche or high-value crops, which require effective marketing strategies to reach consumers. Developing local and regional markets, participating in farmers' markets, and leveraging digital platforms can help farmers connect with buyers who value sustainably produced goods.
- Fair Trade and Ethical Practices - Fair trade and ethical practices are integral to the economic viability of sustainable agriculture. These practices ensure that farmers receive fair compensation for their products, which supports their livelihoods and encourages the adoption of sustainable methods. Fair trade certification and direct trade relationships can provide transparency and trust between producers and consumers.
- Diversification - Diversification is a key strategy for enhancing economic viability. By diversifying crops, livestock, and income streams, farmers can reduce their dependence on a single commodity and spread their financial risk. Diversification can also open up new market opportunities and improve resilience to market fluctuations and environmental challenges.

Social Equity

The principle of social equity addresses the human dimension of sustainable agriculture. It highlights the importance of fair labour practices, community involvement, and equitable access to resources and opportunities. Social equity ensures that the benefits of sustainable agriculture are shared broadly, contributing to the well-being of all stakeholders.

- Labor Rights - Fair labor practices are essential for ensuring the dignity and well-being of agricultural workers. Sustainable agriculture advocates for safe working conditions, fair wages, and the protection of workers' rights. Empowering workers through education and training can also enhance their skills and improve their livelihoods.
- Community Engagement - Community engagement is a cornerstone of social equity in sustainable agriculture. Involving local communities in decision-making processes helps ensure that agricultural practices align with local needs and values. Community-supported agriculture (CSA) programs, cooperative farming, and participatory research are examples of how farmers can collaborate with their communities to achieve common

goals.
- Access to Resources - Equitable access to resources such as land, water, and capital is critical for fostering social equity in agriculture. Policies and programs that support land tenure security, provide affordable credit, and promote gender equality can help marginalized groups participate in and benefit from sustainable agriculture. Ensuring that all farmers have access to the resources they need is essential for creating inclusive and resilient agricultural systems.

Integrated Pest Management (IPM)

Integrated Pest Management is a holistic approach to pest control that emphasizes the use of environmentally friendly methods. IPM combines biological, cultural, physical, and chemical tools to manage pests in a way that minimizes harm to the environment and human health.

- Biological Control - Biological control involves the use of natural enemies, such as predators, parasites, and pathogens, to manage pest populations. This method reduces the reliance on chemical pesticides and promotes ecological balance. Farmers can encourage biological control by creating habitats that support beneficial organisms, such as hedgerows and insectary plants.
- Cultural Practices - Cultural practices are farming techniques that reduce pest pressure through crop management. Examples include crop rotation, intercropping, and planting pest-resistant varieties. These practices disrupt the life cycles of pests and reduce their ability to establish and spread.
- Physical and Mechanical - Control Physical and mechanical control methods involve the use of barriers, traps, and manual removal to manage pests These methods are often simple and cost-effective, making them accessible to small-scale farmers. Examples include the use of row covers to protect crops from insects and hand-picking pests from plants.
- Chemical Control - While chemical control is used as a last resort in IPM, it can be necessary in certain situations. When chemical pesticides are required, sustainable agriculture advocates for the use of selective, low-toxicity products that target specific pests and minimize harm to non-target organisms. Integrated pest management emphasizes the careful monitoring of pest populations to ensure that chemical interventions are used judiciously and responsibly.

Renewable Energy and Resource Efficiency

The principle of renewable energy and resource efficiency focuses on reducing the environmental footprint of agricultural operations. By adopting renewable energy sources and optimizing resource use, sustainable agriculture can mitigate climate change and reduce dependency on non-renewable resources.

- Renewable Energy - Renewable energy sources, such as solar, wind, and biomass, offer sustainable alternatives to fossil fuels. Farmers can harness these energy sources to power irrigation systems, machinery, and processing facilities. Renewable energy not only reduces greenhouse gas emissions but also provides a stable and often more affordable energy supply.
- Resource Efficiency - Resource efficiency involves the careful management of inputs such as water, energy, and nutrients to minimize waste and maximize productivity. Precision agriculture technologies, such as GPS-guided equipment and remote sensing, enable farmers to apply inputs more accurately and efficiently. These technologies help reduce input costs, improve yields, and lessen environmental impacts.
- Climate Resilience - Climate resilience is a critical aspect of sustainable agriculture, as it addresses the ability of agricultural systems to adapt to and withstand the impacts of climate change. Building climate resilience involves implementing practices that enhance the adaptive capacity of farms and communities.
- Adaptive Farming Practices - Adaptive farming practices are techniques that help farmers respond to changing climate conditions. Examples include altering planting dates, selecting drought-tolerant crop varieties, and implementing water conservation measures. These practices enable farmers to maintain productivity in the face of climate variability.
- Risk Management - Risk management strategies are essential for building climate resilience. These strategies include diversifying crops and income sources, investing in crop insurance, and establishing emergency response plans. By anticipating and preparing for climate-related risks, farmers can reduce their vulnerability and enhance their ability to recover from adverse events.
- Research and Innovation - Ongoing research and innovation are vital for developing new solutions to climate challenges. Collaborations between farmers, researchers, and policymakers can drive the development of climate-resilient technologies and practices. Extension services and

knowledge-sharing platforms play a crucial role in disseminating this information to farmers.

The key principles of sustainable agriculture provide a comprehensive framework for creating agricultural systems that are environmentally sound, economically viable, and socially equitable. By adhering to these principles, farmers, policymakers, and stakeholders can work together to ensure that agriculture not only meets the needs of the present but also secures a sustainable future for generations to come.

Sustainable agriculture is not a static concept; it is a dynamic and evolving practice that requires continuous learning, adaptation, and collaboration. As we move forward, it is essential to remain committed to these principles and to strive for innovative solutions that enhance the sustainability and resilience of our agricultural systems.

1.3 Technological Innovations Driving Sustainability

Precision Agriculture: Maximizing Efficiency and Minimizing Waste
Precision agriculture, often referred to as 'smart farming,' is revolutionizing the way we approach crop management. By leveraging advanced technologies such as GPS, IoT sensors, and data analytics, farmers can optimize their use of resources, thereby reducing waste and increasing yield. For instance, GPS-guided tractors can plant seeds with pinpoint accuracy, ensuring optimal spacing and depth. IoT sensors scattered across fields can monitor soil moisture, temperature, and nutrient levels in real-time, enabling farmers to make data-driven decisions about irrigation and fertilization.

One of the most significant benefits of precision agriculture is its ability to reduce the environmental impact of farming. By applying water, fertilizers, and pesticides only where they are needed, in the exact amounts required, and at the right time, precision agriculture minimizes runoff and leaching into surrounding ecosystems. This targeted approach not only conserves vital resources but also protects local wildlife and water sources from contamination.

Moreover, precision agriculture enhances the economic sustainability of farming operations. By improving efficiency and reducing input costs, farmers can achieve higher profit margins. The integration of machine learning algorithms to predict crop yields and optimize planting schedules further adds to the financial viability of sustainable farming practices.

Drones and Aerial Imaging: Eyes in the Sky

Drones equipped with high-resolution cameras and multispectral sensors are becoming increasingly common in modern agriculture. These unmanned aerial vehicles (UAVs) provide a bird's-eye view of fields, capturing detailed images that can be analysed to assess crop health, detect pest infestations, and identify areas of nutrient deficiency.

Aerial imaging allows for early detection of issues that might otherwise go unnoticed until they cause significant damage. For example, a drone can identify patches of crops suffering from disease or pest attacks before they spread, allowing for targeted intervention. This proactive approach not only saves crops but also reduces the need for widespread pesticide application, contributing to a more sustainable farming environment.

Drones also play a crucial role in large-scale land management. For extensive farms, manually scouting fields is time-consuming and labour-intensive. Drones can cover vast areas quickly and efficiently, providing farmers with comprehensive data that can be used to make informed decisions about crop rotation, soil management, and resource allocation.

Artificial Intelligence and Machine Learning: The Brains Behind the Operation

Artificial intelligence (AI) and machine learning (ML) are at the forefront of agricultural innovation. These technologies analyse vast amounts of data collected from various sources, including IoT devices, drones, and satellite imagery, to generate actionable insights.

AI-powered platforms can predict weather patterns, forecast crop yields, and even recommend the best times for planting and harvesting. By analysing historical data and real-time information, these systems help farmers mitigate risks associated with climate variability and market fluctuations. For instance, an AI system can alert a farmer to an impending drought and suggest drought-resistant crop varieties or alternative irrigation strategies.

Machine learning algorithms are also being used to develop advanced pest and disease detection systems. By training models on thousands of images of healthy and diseased plants, researchers have created tools that can identify specific ailments with remarkable accuracy. These systems enable early intervention, reducing crop losses and minimizing the need for chemical treatments.

Robotics and Automation: The Future of Farm Labor

The labour-intensive nature of traditional farming is one of the significant barriers to sustainability. Robotics and automation are addressing this challenge by performing repetitive and physically demanding tasks with greater efficiency and precision.

Automated machinery, such as robotic harvesters, can work around the clock, increasing productivity and reducing labour costs. These machines are equipped with advanced sensors and AI algorithms that allow them to identify ripe produce, pick it gently to avoid damage, and sort it based on quality.

In addition to harvesting, robots are being used for planting, weeding, and even livestock management. Autonomous drones are being developed to plant seeds at a rapid pace, while robotic weeders use machine vision to distinguish between crops and weeds, removing the latter without the need for herbicides. In livestock farming, robotic milking systems can handle the milking process with minimal human intervention, improving animal welfare and reducing labour demands.

Blockchain Technology: Ensuring Transparency and Traceability

Blockchain technology is transforming the way agricultural supply chains operate by providing a secure and transparent method of recording transactions. Each step of the supply chain, from farm to table, can be documented on a blockchain ledger, ensuring traceability and accountability.

For consumers, blockchain offers the assurance that the food they purchase is sustainably sourced and ethically produced. By scanning a QR code on a product's packaging, consumers can access detailed information about the product's journey, including where it was grown, how it was processed, and the conditions under which it was transported.

For farmers and producers, blockchain provides a way to verify certifications and compliance with sustainable practices. It also facilitates direct transactions between farmers and consumers, reducing the need for intermediaries and increasing profit margins for producers.

Furthermore, blockchain can help address issues related to food safety and fraud. In the event of a contamination outbreak, blockchain records can quickly pinpoint the source, enabling rapid response and minimizing public health risks. By ensuring the authenticity of organic and fair-trade certifications, blockchain also helps combat fraud and build consumer trust.

Vertical Farming: Growing Upwards, Not Outwards

Vertical farming is an innovative approach to agriculture that involves growing crops in stacked layers or vertically inclined surfaces, often within controlled indoor environments. This method offers several sustainability benefits, particularly in urban areas where arable land is scarce.

By utilizing vertical space, this farming technique maximizes the use of available land and significantly increases crop yield per square foot. Controlled environment agriculture (CEA) systems used in vertical farms allow for precise regulation of temperature, humidity, and light, creating optimal growing conditions year-round. This results in higher productivity and reduced dependency on seasonal variations.

Vertical farming also greatly reduces water usage compared to traditional farming methods. Closed-loop hydroponic or aeroponic systems recycle water and nutrients, minimizing waste and conserving this precious resource. Additionally, the proximity of vertical farms to urban centres reduces the need for long-distance transportation, lowering carbon emissions associated with food distribution.

Gene Editing and Biotechnology: Tailoring Crops for Sustainability

Advances in gene editing and biotechnology hold immense potential for creating crops that are more resilient, nutritious, and environmentally friendly. Techniques like CRISPR-Cas9 allow scientists to make precise modifications to a plant's DNA, enhancing desirable traits and eliminating harmful ones.

Gene editing can be used to develop crops that are resistant to pests and diseases, reducing the need for chemical pesticides. It can also create drought-tolerant or salt-tolerant varieties, enabling agriculture in regions with challenging growing conditions. These innovations contribute to food security and reduce the environmental impact of farming.

Biotechnology is also being used to enhance the nutritional content of crops.

For example, biofortification can increase the levels of essential vitamins and minerals in staple crops, addressing nutrient deficiencies in populations that rely heavily on these foods.

However, the adoption of gene editing and biotechnology in agriculture is not without its challenges. Ethical considerations, regulatory hurdles, and public perception are significant factors that must be navigated. Nevertheless, with careful management and transparent communication, these technologies have the potential to drive substantial sustainability gains.

Renewable Energy Integration: Powering Sustainable Farms

Integrating renewable energy sources into agricultural operations is a critical aspect of sustainable farming. Solar panels, wind turbines, and biomass energy systems can provide farms with clean, renewable power, reducing reliance on fossil fuels and lowering greenhouse gas emissions.

Solar energy is particularly well-suited for agriculture. Solar panels can be installed on rooftops, over-irrigation canals, or even in fields without taking up valuable cropland. Solar-powered irrigation systems can efficiently pump water from wells or reservoirs, reducing the energy costs associated with traditional irrigation methods.

Wind energy is another viable option, especially in regions with consistent wind patterns. Small-scale wind turbines can generate electricity for farm operations, while larger turbines can contribute to the local power grid, providing an additional revenue stream for farmers.

Biomass energy, derived from agricultural waste products like crop residues and animal manure, offers a sustainable way to manage farm waste while generating power. Anaerobic digesters can convert organic waste into biogas, which can be used for heating, electricity generation, or as a vehicle fuel.

This demand can only grow into the future as transportation and machinery energy sources move from fossil fuels to electrification. Farm-based wind generation is anticipated to, eventually, supply green hydrogen to charge fuel cells on tractors and haulage equipment around the farm.

Embracing Innovation for a Sustainable Future

Technological innovations are at the heart of the sustainable agriculture movement. Precision agriculture, drones, AI, robotics, blockchain, vertical farming, gene editing, and renewable energy integration are transforming how we grow food, making it more efficient, resilient, and environmentally friendly.

However, implementing these technologies requires collaboration between farmers, researchers, policymakers, and investors. By embracing innovation and fostering a supportive ecosystem, we can create a sustainable agricultural future that meets the needs of a growing global population while preserving the health of our planet.

The journey towards sustainable agriculture is ongoing, and the innovations discussed in this chapter are just the beginning. As technology evolves, new opportunities that offer even greater potential for positive impact will arise. By staying informed and adaptable, we can ensure that agriculture thrives in harmony with the environment, securing a sustainable harvest for generations not yet born.

1.4 Pioneering Paths: Case Studies - Sustainable Agricultural Practices

Paving the Way for Sustainability
The journey to sustainable agriculture is rich with stories of innovation, resilience, and transformation. This section delves into remarkable case studies that highlight successful sustainable agricultural practices from around the globe. These stories serve as both inspiration and practical examples for policymakers, investors, and entrepreneurs looking to foster a greener, more resilient agricultural ecosystem.

<u>The Regenerative Revolution: Gabe Brown's Farm in North Dakota</u>

Gabe Brown's farm in North Dakota stands as a beacon of regenerative agriculture. Over the past two decades, Brown has transformed his 5,000-acre farm from a struggling operation into a thriving example of sustainable farming. Focusing on soil health, Brown has implemented practices such as no-till farming, diverse crop rotations, and livestock integration. These methods have not only improved soil fertility but also increased crop yields and profitability.

Key Practices:

1. No-Till Farming: Reduces soil erosion and improves water retention.

2. Diverse Crop Rotations: Enhances soil health and disrupts pest cycles.
3. Livestock Integration: Promotes nutrient cycling and soil fertility.

Outcomes:

- Soil Health: Increased organic matter from 1.7% to over 6%.
- Economic Viability: Reduced input costs by 75%, increasing profitability.
- Environmental Impact: Enhanced biodiversity and reduced carbon footprint.

Scaling Agroforestry: The Example of Fazenda da Toca in Brazil

Fazenda da Toca, an innovative agroforestry project in Brazil, exemplifies the potential of integrating trees with crops and livestock. Founded by Pedro Paulo Diniz, a former Formula 1 driver turned environmentalist, the farm combines sustainable agriculture with reforestation efforts. Spanning over 2,300 hectares, Fazenda da Toca employs a holistic approach to land management, promoting biodiversity, soil health, and economic resilience

Key Practices:

1. Agroforestry Systems: Integrates trees with crops and livestock to enhance ecosystem services.
2. Organic Farming: Eliminates synthetic chemicals, focusing on natural inputs.
3. Biodiversity Corridors: Establishes wildlife corridors to support native species.

Outcomes:

- Soil Health: Improved soil structure and increased carbon sequestration.
- Economic Resilience: Diversified income streams from crops, livestock, and timber.
- Environmental Impact: Restored 1,000 hectares of degraded land and increased biodiversity.

Urban Agriculture: The Success of Gotham Greens in New York City

Gotham Greens has revolutionized urban agriculture with its network of rooftop greenhouses across New York City. By growing fresh produce in controlled environments, Gotham Greens addresses the challenges of urban food security and sustainability. Their hydroponic systems use 95% less water than traditional agriculture and eliminate the need for pesticides and herbicides.

Key Practices:

1. Hydroponic Systems: Utilizes nutrient-rich water solutions for plant growth, reducing water usage.
2. Rooftop Greenhouses: Maximizes urban space and reduces food miles.
3. Renewable Energy: Powers greenhouses with solar panels and other renewable sources.

Outcomes:

- Food Security: Provides fresh, local produce to urban communities year-round.
- Economic Viability: Generates high yields with lower operational costs.
- Environmental Impact: Reduces carbon emissions and urban heat island effect.

Community-Led Transformation: The Case of Navdanya in India

Navdanya, founded by Dr. Vandana Shiva, is a movement promoting biodiversity conservation and organic farming in India. Through its network of seed banks and training programs, Navdanya empowers local farmers to adopt sustainable practices. The initiative has reached over 5 million farmers across 22 states, transforming agricultural landscapes and improving livelihoods.

Key Practices:

1. Seed Banks: Preserve indigenous seed varieties and promote seed sovereignty.
2. Organic Farming: Encourages chemical-free farming methods and traditional knowledge.
3. Farmer Training: Provides education on sustainable practices and market access.

Outcomes:

- Biodiversity Conservation: Preserved over 3,000 rice varieties and other

indigenous crops.
- Economic Empowerment: Increased farmer incomes by 30-60% through organic certification and direct markets.
- Environmental Impact: Reduced dependency on chemical inputs and improved soil health.

High-Tech Sustainability: The Role of Vertical Farms Like AeroFarms

AeroFarms, based in Newark, New Jersey, is a leading example of high-tech vertical farming. By utilizing aeroponic technology, AeroFarms grows leafy greens in vertically stacked layers without soil. This method uses 95% less water and 99% less land than traditional farming, making it a highly sustainable solution for urban agriculture.

Key Practices:

1. Aeroponic Technology: Delivers nutrients directly to plant roots through mist, optimizing water and nutrient use.

2. LED Lighting: Mimics natural sunlight to stimulate plant growth and energy efficiency.

3. Data-Driven Farming: Uses sensors and AI to monitor and optimize growing conditions

Outcomes:

- Resource Efficiency: Significantly reduced water and land usage.

- High Yields: Produces up to 390 times more food per square foot compared to traditional farming.

- Environmental Impact: Minimizes carbon footprint and eliminates the need for pesticides.

Cooperative Success: The Mondragon Corporation's Agricultural Initiatives

The Mondragon Corporation, a federation of worker cooperatives in Spain, includes several agricultural cooperatives that exemplify sustainable practices. Through democratic management and community involvement, these cooperatives focus on organic farming, renewable energy, and fair trade, contributing to both economic and environmental sustainability.

Key Practices:

1. Cooperative Governance: Ensures democratic decision-making and profit-sharing among members.
2. Organic Farming: Prioritizes sustainable methods and certified organic products.
3. Renewable Energy: Utilizes solar and wind power to reduce carbon emissions.

Outcomes:

- Economic Resilience: Provides stable incomes and employment for cooperative members.
- Environmental Stewardship: Reduces environmental impact through sustainable practices.
- Community Empowerment: Strengthens local economies and fosters social cohesion.

Lessons Learned and the Way Forward

These case studies illustrate the diverse approaches and impact of sustainable agricultural practices. From regenerative farming in North Dakota to high-tech vertical farms in New Jersey, the common thread is a commitment to environmental stewardship, economic viability, and social responsibility. As we move forward, these examples provide valuable insights and a roadmap for scaling sustainable agriculture globally. By learning from these pioneers, we can foster a more resilient and sustainable future for agriculture.

- Sustainable agriculture is not a one-size-fits-all approach but a multifaceted strategy that evolves with each generation.
- The future of farming lies in the harmonious integration of advanced technology and age-old sustainable practices.

- True sustainability in agriculture is achieved when we can meet today's needs without compromising the ability of future generations to meet theirs.

Sustainable agriculture is grounded in the principles of environmental stewardship, economic profitability, and social responsibility. It requires a comprehensive approach that balances these three pillars to ensure long-term viability.

Technological innovations such as precision farming, biotechnology, and renewable energy sources are crucial in advancing sustainable agriculture. These innovations not only enhance productivity but also minimize environmental impact and promote resource efficiency.

The Path Forward for Sustainable Agriculture

As we reflect on the evolution of sustainable agriculture, it is clear that we have come a long way from the traditional farming methods that once dominated the landscape. The shift towards practices that prioritize environmental stewardship, economic viability, and social responsibility has set the stage for a more resilient and sustainable agricultural future.

Key principles such as crop rotation, integrated pest management, and conservation tillage have emerged as cornerstones of this movement, ensuring that farming practices are not only productive but also sustainable for generations to come.

Technological innovations have played a pivotal role in driving this transformation. From precision farming and advanced irrigation systems to the use of renewable energy and biotechnology, these advancements have significantly enhanced the efficiency and sustainability of agricultural operations. They have enabled farmers to optimize resource use, reduce waste, and minimize the environmental impact of their activities.

The use of case studies of successful sustainable agricultural practices provide practical insights and inspiration for others to follow. They demonstrate that sustainability is not just a theoretical concept but a viable and rewarding approach to farming. These examples highlight the importance of adopting a holistic and adaptive mindset, one that embraces change and continuously seeks to improve.

In conclusion, the journey towards sustainable agriculture is ongoing, and it requires the collective effort of all stakeholders. Farmers, policymakers, researchers, and consumers all have a role to play in supporting and advancing sustainable practices

By staying informed, embracing innovation, and committing to the principles of sustainability, we can ensure a thriving agricultural sector that meets the needs of the present without compromising the ability of future generations to meet their own. Let this chapter serve as a reminder of the progress we have made and a call to action for the work that still lies ahead.

Welcome to the journey of sustainable management.

2 ENVIRONMENTAL, SOCIAL, AND GOVERNANCE (ESG) IN AGRICULTURE

Source: Pexels - Photo by NC Farm Bureau

In the modern era, the landscape of agriculture is undergoing a seismic transformation. As the world grapples with climate change, resource scarcity, and social inequities, the principles of Environmental, Social, and Governance (ESG) have emerged as a pivotal framework for fostering sustainable and resilient agricultural practices.

ESG is not just a set of guidelines; it is a comprehensive approach that integrates environmental stewardship, social responsibility, and ethical governance into the core of agricultural enterprises.

This chapter delves into the nuanced relationship between ESG and agriculture, elucidating its significance and the revolutionary impact it holds for the future of farming. ESG in agriculture is about more than just adhering to regulatory requirements; it represents a holistic strategy to achieve long-term sustainability and profitability for the farm as a business. At its core, ESG in agriculture seeks to harmonize the objectives of economic viability with the imperatives of environmental conservation and social equity.

This chapter will guide you through the intricate layers of ESG, starting with a clear definition and its relevance to the agricultural sector.

The environmental component of ESG focuses on mitigating the adverse impacts of farming activities on our planet. Agriculture, as both a significant contributor to and a potential mitigator of climate change, holds a unique position. Here, we will explore how sustainable agricultural practices can reduce carbon footprints, conserve biodiversity, and promote ecological balance. From precision farming to regenerative agriculture, innovative strategies are being deployed to ensure that agriculture contributes positively to the environment rather than depleting its resources.

Social responsibility within the ESG framework addresses the human element of agriculture. The labour force, often the unsung heroes of the agricultural supply chain, is central to this discussion. Ensuring fair labour practices, safe working conditions, and community engagement are not just ethical imperatives but are also essential for the sustainability of the agricultural sector. This chapter will highlight case studies where social responsibility initiatives have led to enhanced productivity and community well-being, demonstrating that social equity and business success can go hand in hand.

Governance, the third pillar of ESG, is about establishing transparent, accountable, and ethical management practices within agricultural enterprises. Good governance is foundational to building trust with stakeholders, including consumers, investors, and regulatory bodies. This section will delve into best practices for corporate governance in agriculture, illustrating how ethical management can drive both compliance and competitive advantage. Whether through transparent reporting, stakeholder engagement, or robust risk management, governance practices are critical to the integrity and success of agricultural ventures.

As we unpack the components of ESG in agriculture, it becomes evident that this framework is not just a trend but a necessary evolution for the industry. The convergence of environmental stewardship, social responsibility, and ethical governance offers a roadmap for transforming agriculture into a force for good. This chapter aims to equip policymakers, investors, and entrepreneurs with the insights and strategies needed to navigate this complex but rewarding landscape.

Embracing ESG principles allows us to pave the way to a more sustainable harvest that will benefit not only our bottom line but also the planet. Join us as we explore the transformative power of ESG in agriculture. This chapter is written to provide a comprehensive understanding of how integrating ESG principles can revolutionise farming practices, drive sustainable growth, and create a resilient agricultural ecosystem. Together, we will uncover the potential at the intersection of agriculture and ESG, and envision a future where sustainable harvests are the norm rather than the exception.

2.1 The Pillars of ESG: A Framework for Sustainability

In recent years, the concept of Environmental, Social, and Governance (ESG) has emerged as a critical framework for evaluating the sustainability and ethical impact of various industries, including agriculture.

ESG criteria are a set of standards for a company's operations that socially conscious investors use to screen potential investments. In the context of agriculture, ESG principles serve as a comprehensive guide to sustainable farming practices that not only protect the environment but also address social responsibilities and promote ethical governance.

Environmental Aspects: Stewardship of Natural Resources

The environmental component of ESG in agriculture focuses on the stewardship of natural resources. This includes practices that minimize environmental impact, such as reducing greenhouse gas emissions, conserving water, and maintaining soil health. Sustainable agriculture practices like crop rotation, organic farming, and integrated pest management are essential. These practices not only enhance productivity but also ensure the long-term viability of the land.

Reducing Greenhouse Gas Emissions
Agriculture is a significant contributor to greenhouse gas emissions, accounting for approximately 10-12% of global emissions. Sustainable practices like no-till farming, cover cropping, and the use of biochar can significantly reduce emissions. Additionally, adopting renewable energy sources such as solar and wind power for farm operations can further mitigate the carbon footprint of agricultural activities.

Water Conservation
Water is a critical resource in agriculture, and its efficient use is vital for sustainability. Techniques such as drip irrigation, rainwater harvesting, and drought-resistant crop varieties can help conserve water. Precision agriculture technologies, which use data analytics and IoT devices to optimise water usage, are increasingly being adopted to enhance water efficiency.

Soil Health
Healthy soil is the foundation of sustainable agriculture. Practices like crop rotation, cover cropping, and reduced tillage help maintain soil structure, fertility, and biodiversity. These approaches prevent soil erosion and enhance its ability to sequester carbon, contributing to climate change mitigation.

Social Aspects: Building Resilient Communities

The social dimension of ESG in agriculture focuses on the well-being of communities involved in or affected by agricultural activities. This includes ensuring fair labour practices, promoting gender equality, and supporting local economies. Social sustainability in agriculture also improves food security and nutrition, which are essential for the health and prosperity of communities.

Fair Labor Practices
Agricultural labour is often associated with challenging working conditions and low wages. Ensuring fair labour practices means providing safe working conditions, fair wages, and access to benefits for farmworkers. Certification programs like Fair Trade and Rainforest Alliance set standards for labour practices and help consumers make informed choices.

Gender Equality
Women play a crucial role in agriculture, yet they often face significant barriers to accessing resources and decision-making opportunities. Promoting gender equality includes giving women equal access to land, credit, and education. Empowering women farmers can lead to increased agricultural productivity and improved community well-being.

Strengthening Local Economies
Sustainable agriculture can drive economic development in rural areas. Supporting local farmers, businesses and communities can build more resilient economies. This includes initiatives like farmers' markets, community-supported agriculture (CSA), and cooperatives, which provide farmers with better market access and consumers with fresh, local produce.

Governance Aspects: Ethical and Transparent Practices

The governance component of ESG in agriculture addresses the ethical and transparent management of agricultural enterprises. This includes corporate governance practices, stakeholder engagement, and compliance with regulations. Good governance ensures that agricultural practices are aligned with broader community and societal goals and contribute to sustainable development.

Corporate Governance
Effective corporate governance in agriculture involves setting clear policies and procedures to ensure accountability, transparency, and ethical behaviour. This includes the establishment of boards of directors, audit committees, and compliance programs to oversee operations and ensure that they adhere to legal and ethical standards.

Stakeholder Engagement
Engaging with stakeholders, including farmers, consumers, investors, and local communities, is essential for sustainable agriculture. This involves regular communication, consultation, and collaboration to address their concerns and incorporate their feedback into decision-making processes. Stakeholder engagement helps build trust and ensures that agricultural practices meet the needs and expectations of all involved parties.

Compliance and Reporting
Compliance with environmental, social, and governance regulations is a critical aspect of sustainable agriculture. This includes adhering to local, national, and international laws and standards. Transparent reporting of ESG performance, through sustainability reports and other disclosures, helps stakeholders assess the impact of agricultural practices and hold companies accountable.

Integrating ESG into Agricultural Practices

Integrating ESG principles into agricultural practices requires a holistic approach that considers the interconnectedness of environmental, social, and governance factors. This involves adopting sustainable farming techniques, ensuring fair treatment of workers, and maintaining ethical business practices. By embedding ESG into their operations, agricultural enterprises can enhance their resilience, improve their market competitiveness, and contribute to sustainable development.

Sustainable Farming Techniques
Adopting sustainable farming techniques is the cornerstone of ESG in agriculture. This includes practices like agroforestry, organic farming, and regenerative agriculture, which promote biodiversity, enhance soil health, and reduce environmental impact. Precision agriculture technologies, such as satellite imagery and data analytics, can optimize resource use and improve crop yields.

Fair Treatment of Workers
Ensuring fair treatment of workers involves providing safe working conditions, fair wages, and opportunities for skill development. This not only improves labour productivity but also enhances the social sustainability of agricultural enterprises. Certification programs and partnerships with labour organizations can help ensure compliance with fair labour standards.

Ethical Business Practices
Maintaining ethical business practices involves transparency, accountability, and responsible decision-making. This includes fair pricing, ethical sourcing,

and responsible marketing. Companies can implement codes of conduct and ethical guidelines to ensure that their business practices align with ESG principles.

The Future of ESG in Agriculture

The integration of ESG principles into agriculture is not just a trend but a necessity for the future of the industry. As global challenges like climate change, food insecurity, and social inequality continue to intensify, the adoption of ESG practices will play a crucial role in addressing these issues. The future of agriculture lies in sustainable practices that balance economic viability with environmental stewardship and social responsibility.

Climate Change Mitigation and Adaptation
Climate change poses significant risks to agriculture, including extreme weather events, changing precipitation patterns, and rising temperatures. ESG practices can help mitigate these risks by promoting climate-smart agriculture, enhancing resilience, and reducing greenhouse gas emissions. This includes adopting climate-resilient crop varieties, improving water management, and enhancing soil health.

Enhancing Food Security
Sustainable agriculture practices that align with ESG principles can enhance food security by increasing agricultural productivity, improving food distribution, and reducing food waste. This involves adopting innovative technologies, supporting smallholder farmers, and improving supply chain efficiency. By ensuring a stable and sustainable food supply, ESG practices contribute to global food security.

Promoting Social Equity
ESG practices in agriculture can promote social equity by addressing issues such as fair labour practices, gender equality, and community development. This involves providing equitable access to resources, opportunities, and benefits for all stakeholders, including marginalized and vulnerable populations. Promoting social equity enhances the social sustainability of agricultural enterprises and contributes to broader societal goals.

Charting a Sustainable Future

The integration of ESG principles into agriculture is a powerful framework for fostering sustainable development. By addressing environmental, social, and governance factors, agricultural enterprises can enhance their resilience, improve their market competitiveness, and contribute to a more sustainable and equitable future. As we move forward, the adoption of ESG practices will be essential for meeting the global challenges of climate change, food insecurity, and social inequality. By embracing ESG principles, we can chart a sustainable future for agriculture and ensure a resilient and thriving food system for generations to come.

2.2 Reducing Carbon Footprint and Conserving Biodiversity: A Dual Mandate for Sustainable Agriculture

The convergence of agriculture and Environmental, Social, and Governance (ESG) principles embodies a transformative approach poised to redefine the future of food production. Within this expansive framework, reducing the carbon footprint and conserving biodiversity emerge as two pivotal objectives. These elements not only contribute to mitigating climate change but also ensure the ecological balance necessary for sustainable agricultural practices. In this section, we look into the strategies, practices, and innovations driving these objectives, offering a comprehensive understanding of their critical importance and practical implementation.

The Importance of Reducing Carbon Footprint in Agriculture

Agriculture is a significant contributor to global greenhouse gas emissions, accounting for approximately 24% of total emissions when considering land use and deforestation. This varies however and in Ireland for example, agriculture was responsible for 37.8% of greenhouse gas emissions in 2023. The carbon footprint of agricultural activities encompasses various sources, including methane emissions from livestock, nitrous oxide from fertilized soils, and carbon dioxide from the use of fossil fuels in machinery and transportation. Reducing this footprint is crucial for achieving global climate targets and ensuring the long-term viability of agricultural systems.

Strategies for Reducing Carbon Footprint

Adoption of Precision Agriculture

Precision agriculture leverages technology to optimize field-level management with regard to crop farming. By utilizing data-driven insights from satellite imagery, GPS, and IoT sensors, farmers can apply inputs such as water, fertilizers, and pesticides more efficiently. This minimizes waste, reduces the over-application of chemicals, and lowers greenhouse gas emissions. Precision agriculture not only enhances productivity but also contributes to environmental sustainability.

Transition to Renewable Energy Sources

Agricultural operations are energy-intensive, relying heavily on fossil fuels for machinery, irrigation, and transportation. Transitioning to renewable energy sources such as solar, wind, and bioenergy can significantly reduce the carbon footprint. Solar-powered irrigation systems, for example, provide a sustainable alternative to diesel-powered pumps, reducing emissions and operational costs.

Implementation of Conservation Tillage
Conservation tillage, including no-till and reduced-till practices, minimizes soil disturbance, preserving soil organic carbon and reducing carbon dioxide emissions. These practices also improve soil health, water retention, and biodiversity. By maintaining a permanent soil cover, conservation tillage enhances carbon sequestration and contributes to climate resilience.

Integration of Agroforestry Systems
Agroforestry, the practice of integrating trees and shrubs into agricultural landscapes, offers multiple benefits. Trees sequester carbon, enhance biodiversity, and improve soil structure. Agroforestry systems can also provide additional income through the production of timber, fruits, and other non-timber forest products. This integrated approach promotes a diversified and resilient agricultural system.

Case Studies in Carbon Footprint Reduction

The Role of Precision Agriculture in Reducing Emissions
A study conducted in the Midwest United States demonstrated that precision agriculture practices reduced nitrogen fertilizer use by 20%, resulting in a 10% reduction in nitrous oxide emissions. The use of variable-rate technology for fertilizer application ensured that crops received the right amount of nutrients, minimizing environmental impact.

Solar-Powered Irrigation in India
In India, the introduction of solar-powered irrigation systems has transformed agricultural practices in regions with limited access to electricity. These systems have reduced reliance on diesel pumps, cutting carbon dioxide emissions and lowering irrigation costs. Farmers have reported increased crop yields and improved water management as a result.

Conserving Biodiversity: A Cornerstone of Sustainable Agriculture

Biodiversity is the foundation of resilient agricultural systems. It encompasses the variety of life forms within an ecosystem, including plants, animals, microorganisms, and their genetic diversity. Conserving biodiversity enhances ecosystem services such as pollination, pest control, and nutrient cycling, which are essential for sustainable agriculture.

Strategies for Conserving Biodiversity

Promoting Crop Diversity

Monoculture, the cultivation of a single crop species over a large area, can lead to soil degradation, pest outbreaks, and reduced resilience to climate change. Promoting crop diversity through polyculture and crop rotation enhances soil health, reduces pest pressures, and improves overall ecosystem stability. Diverse cropping systems also provide habitat for beneficial organisms and contribute to a balanced agroecosystem.

Establishing Biodiversity Corridors

Biodiversity corridors are areas of natural habitat that connect fragmented landscapes, allowing wildlife to move freely and maintain genetic diversity. Establishing these corridors within agricultural lands supports the movement of pollinators, predators, and other beneficial species. These corridors can include hedgerows, riparian buffers, and forest patches, creating a mosaic of habitats that enhance biodiversity.

Implementing Integrated Pest Management (IPM)

Integrated Pest Management (IPM) is an ecological approach to pest control that combines biological, cultural, mechanical, and chemical methods. By prioritizing natural pest control mechanisms, IPM reduces the reliance on synthetic pesticides, which can harm non-target species and disrupt ecosystem balance. IPM strategies include the use of beneficial insects, crop rotation, and habitat manipulation to manage pest populations sustainably.

Protecting and Restoring Natural Habitats

Protecting existing natural habitats and restoring degraded ones is crucial for conserving biodiversity. Wetlands, forests, and grasslands provide essential ecosystem services and serve as reservoirs of genetic diversity. Restoration efforts can include reforestation, wetland rehabilitation, and the establishment of conservation easements to safeguard critical habitats.

Case Studies in Biodiversity Conservation

The Impact of Crop Diversity in Mexico

In Mexico, traditional milpa systems, which involve the intercropping of maize, beans, and squash, have demonstrated the benefits of crop diversity. These systems enhance soil fertility, reduce pest pressures, and provide a diverse range of food products. The milpa system's resilience to climate variability underscores the importance of crop diversity in sustainable agriculture.

Biodiversity Corridors in Brazil's Atlantic Forest
In Brazil, the creation of biodiversity corridors within the Atlantic Forest has reconnected fragmented habitats, allowing wildlife to thrive. These corridors have supported the movement of pollinators and seed dispersers, contributing to forest regeneration and biodiversity conservation. The project has also engaged local communities in conservation efforts, highlighting the social dimension of biodiversity preservation.

The Synergy: Carbon Reduction and Biodiversity Conservation

Reducing the carbon footprint and conserving biodiversity are not mutually exclusive goals. They often reinforce each other, creating a synergistic effect that enhances the overall sustainability of agricultural systems. Practices such as agroforestry, conservation tillage, and crop diversity simultaneously sequester carbon and support biodiversity.

Agroforestry: A Dual Benefit
Agroforestry systems exemplify the synergy between carbon reduction and biodiversity conservation. By integrating trees into agricultural landscapes, these systems sequester carbon, improve soil health, and provide habitat for diverse species. The presence of trees enhances microclimates, supports pollinators, and reduces the need for chemical inputs, creating a more resilient and sustainable agroecosystem.

Conservation Tillage: Enhancing Soil Carbon and Biodiversity
Conservation tillage practices, such as no-till and reduced-till, preserve soil structure and organic matter, enhancing carbon sequestration. These practices also create a favourable environment for soil organisms, promoting biodiversity below ground. Earthworms, beneficial microbes, and other soil fauna thrive in undisturbed soils, contributing to nutrient cycling and soil health.

The intersection of reducing carbon footprint and conserving biodiversity is a critical component of sustainable agriculture. By adopting practices that address both objectives, farmers can contribute to climate mitigation, enhance ecosystem resilience, and ensure the long-term viability of agricultural systems. The journey towards a sustainable harvest requires a holistic approach that integrates environmental stewardship, technological innovation, and community engagement. As we navigate the future of agriculture, the dual mandate of carbon reduction and biodiversity conservation will remain at the forefront of our collective efforts to create a greener, more resilient food system.

2.3 Social Responsibility: Labour & Community Engagement

In the quest for a greener and more sustainable agricultural sector, the human element often takes centre stage. At the heart of Environmental, Social, and Governance (ESG) principles lies a commitment to social responsibility, which emphasizes fair labour practices and robust community engagement.

This section delves deep into the social dimensions of sustainable agriculture, exploring how ethical labour practices and meaningful community involvement are not just moral imperatives but also essential components for long-term success and sustainability.

The Importance of Fair Labor Practices

Historically, agriculture has been an industry fraught with labour exploitation, from the use of child labour to unsafe working conditions and unfair wages. The push for sustainability cannot turn a blind eye to these issues. Instead, it must actively work to rectify them. Fair labour practices are not merely about compliance with laws and regulations; they aim to ensure that workers are treated with dignity and respect, which in turn can lead to increased productivity and loyalty.

Ethical Standards and Certifications
One way to ensure fair labour practices is through adherence to ethical standards and certifications. Organizations like Fair Trade and Rainforest Alliance have set rigorous criteria that address workers' rights, wages, and working conditions. Achieving these certifications can not only improve the lives of farmworkers but also enhance a farm's reputation and marketability. Consumers are increasingly willing to pay a premium for products that are ethically sourced, making fair labour practices a sound business strategy as well.

Fair Trade Coffee
Consider the case of Fair Trade coffee. Farmers who participate in Fair Trade programs receive a guaranteed minimum price for their coffee beans, which protects them from market volatility. Additionally, these programs often include community development premiums, which are invested in local projects like schools and healthcare facilities. The result is a more stable and prosperous community, demonstrating the far-reaching benefits of fair labour practices.

Engagement: Building Stronger, Healthier Communities

The Role of Community in Sustainable Agriculture
Community engagement is another cornerstone of social responsibility in agriculture. Sustainable farming practices are most effective when they are

integrated into the local community. This means involving community members in decision-making processes, respecting local traditions, and contributing to community well-being.

Participatory Approaches
Participatory approaches to community engagement involve local stakeholders in planning and implementing agricultural projects. This can range from community meetings and focus groups to more formal advisory boards. By giving community members a voice, farms can ensure that their practices align with local needs and values. This not only fosters goodwill but also leads to more effective and sustainable outcomes.

Community-Supported Agriculture (CSA)
Community-supported agriculture (CSA) programs are a prime example of effective community engagement. In a CSA, consumers purchase shares of a farm's harvest in advance, providing farmers with upfront capital and a guaranteed market. In return, consumers receive a regular supply of fresh, locally-grown produce. This model strengthens the bond between farmers and consumers, fosters a sense of community, and promotes sustainable farming practices.

The Interplay Between Fair Labor Practices and Community Engagement

Synergistic Benefits
Fair labour practices and community engagement are not isolated components of social responsibility; they are deeply interconnected. Fair labour practices contribute to community well-being by ensuring that workers receive fair wages and safe working conditions. In turn, a strong community can support sustainable agriculture by providing a stable, engaged workforce and a market for sustainably produced goods.

Holistic Approaches
A holistic approach to social responsibility in agriculture recognizes the interplay between fair labour practices and community engagement. For example, a farm might implement a worker-cooperative model, where employees have a stake in the business and participate in decision-making. This not only ensures fair labour practices but also fosters a sense of community and collective responsibility.

Challenges and Solutions

Overcoming Barriers to Fair Labor Practices
Implementing fair labour practices can be challenging, especially for small farms with limited resources. However, several solutions can help overcome

these barriers. For instance, farms can form cooperatives to share resources and achieve economies of scale. Governments and NGOs can also provide support through grants, training programs, and technical assistance.

Addressing Community Engagement Challenges
Community engagement can also present challenges, such as language barriers, cultural differences, and resistance to change. Effective communication is key to overcoming these obstacles. Farms can employ community liaisons or facilitators who understand the local culture and can bridge gaps between farmers and community members. Additionally, ongoing education and outreach efforts can help build trust and encourage community participation.

Future Directions

The Role of Technology
Technology can play a significant role in enhancing fair labour practices and community engagement. For example, blockchain technology can be used to create transparent supply chains, ensuring that labour practices are fair and ethical from farm to table. Social media and other digital platforms can facilitate communication and engagement with local communities, providing a forum for feedback and collaboration.

Policy Implications
Policymakers have a crucial role to play in promoting social responsibility in agriculture. This can include enacting and enforcing labour laws, providing incentives for fair labour practices, and supporting community engagement initiatives. By creating a favourable policy environment, governments can help ensure that sustainable agriculture practices are both socially responsible and economically viable.

As we move towards a more sustainable agricultural sector, the importance of social responsibility cannot be overstated. Fair labor practices and community engagement are not just ethical imperatives; they are essential components of a sustainable and resilient food system. By prioritizing the well-being of workers and communities, we can create a more equitable and sustainable future for all.

2.4 Governance: Transparent and Ethical Management in Agriculture

The Foundation of Trust Is Transparency

The cornerstone of any successful agricultural enterprise lies in its governance framework, which must be built upon a foundation of transparency. Transparency in governance refers to the openness and accessibility of information related to the company's operations, financial status, and decision-making processes. This is crucial not only for maintaining the trust of stakeholders but also for fostering a culture of accountability within the organization.

Transparency ensures that all stakeholders, including investors, employees, customers, and the community, are kept informed about the company's activities and performance. This can be achieved through regular reporting, open communication channels, and the use of technology to provide real-time updates. For instance, agricultural enterprises can leverage blockchain technology to track and share information about their supply chains, ensuring that every step of the process is visible and verifiable.

In addition to technological solutions, transparent governance also requires a commitment to ethical practices. This means that companies must be willing to disclose both their successes and their failures and to take responsibility for any negative impacts their operations may have. By doing so, they can build a reputation for integrity and gain the trust of their stakeholders.

Ethical Management: Beyond Compliance

While compliance with laws and regulations is a fundamental aspect of governance, ethical management goes beyond mere adherence to legal requirements. It involves a commitment to doing what is right, even when it is not mandated by law. This can encompass a wide range of practices, from fair labour practices and environmental stewardship to community engagement and corporate social responsibility.

One of the key aspects of ethical management in agriculture is ensuring fair treatment of workers. This includes providing safe working conditions, fair wages, and opportunities for professional development. Companies must also be vigilant in preventing and addressing any forms of exploitation or abuse within their operations.

Environmental stewardship is another critical component of ethical management. Agricultural enterprises have a significant impact on the environment, and it is their responsibility to minimize this impact through sustainable practices. This can include reducing pesticide use, conserving water, and protecting biodiversity. By prioritizing environmental sustainability, companies can not only reduce their ecological footprint but also enhance their reputation as responsible and ethical businesses.

The Role of Governance in Risk Management

Effective governance is essentially managing risk whatever the industry. The agricultural sector is subject to a wide range of risks, including market volatility, climate change, and regulatory changes. A robust governance framework can help companies identify, assess, and mitigate these risks, ensuring their long-term sustainability and resilience.

One of the key components of risk management is the establishment of clear policies and procedures. These should outline the company's approach to risk, including how risks are identified, assessed, and managed. Companies should also have a crisis management plan in place, detailing the steps to be taken in the event of an emergency or unexpected event.

In addition to internal policies, companies must also engage with external stakeholders to manage risks effectively. This can include collaborating with industry associations, government agencies, and non-governmental organizations to share knowledge and resources. By working together, companies can develop more effective strategies for addressing the complex challenges facing the agricultural sector.

The Importance of Stakeholder Engagement

Stakeholder engagement is a critical aspect of governance in agricultural enterprises. Engaging with stakeholders helps companies understand their needs and expectations, and ensures that their interests are taken into account in decision-making processes. This can lead to more informed and inclusive decisions, enhancing the company's reputation and building stronger relationships with stakeholders.

There are many ways to engage with stakeholders, including regular meetings, surveys, and public consultations. Companies can also use social media and other digital platforms to communicate with stakeholders and gather their feedback. It is important to ensure that engagement is ongoing and not limited to specific events or issues.

One of the key benefits of stakeholder engagement is that it can help companies identify emerging trends and issues, allowing them to respond proactively. For example, by engaging with local communities, companies can gain insights into the social and environmental impacts of their operations and take steps to address any concerns. This can help prevent conflicts and build trust with the community.

Governance and Innovation: Driving Sustainable Agriculture

Governance plays a crucial role in fostering innovation in agricultural enterprises. By creating a supportive and transparent environment, companies can encourage creativity and experimentation, leading to the development of new technologies and practices that promote sustainability.

One way to foster innovation is through the establishment of research and development (R&D) programs. These programs can focus on a wide range of areas, from improving crop yields and reducing resource use to developing new products and markets. Companies can also collaborate with universities, research institutions, and other organizations to leverage their expertise and resources.

In addition to R&D, companies can also support innovation by creating a culture that encourages risk-taking and learning from failure. This can involve providing training and development opportunities for employees, as well as recognizing and rewarding innovative ideas and achievements.

Governance can also play a role in scaling up successful innovations. This can involve developing strategies for commercializing new technologies and practices, as well as securing funding and partnerships to support their implementation. By fostering a culture of innovation, companies can drive sustainable agriculture and create long-term value for their stakeholders.

Governance and ESG Reporting: Measuring and Communicating Impact

ESG reporting is an essential component of governance in agricultural enterprises. ESG reporting involves measuring and communicating the company's environmental, social, and governance performance, providing stakeholders with a comprehensive view of its impact and sustainability.

Effective ESG reporting requires the establishment of clear metrics and benchmarks, allowing companies to track their progress and identify areas for improvement. This can include a wide range of indicators, from greenhouse gas emissions and water use to labour practices and community engagement.

In addition to quantitative data, ESG reporting should also include qualitative information, providing context and insights into the company's performance. This can involve sharing case studies, success stories, and lessons learned, helping stakeholders understand the company's efforts and achievements.

Transparency is key to effective ESG reporting. Companies must be willing to disclose both their successes and challenges, providing a balanced and honest view of their performance. This can help build trust with stakeholders and demonstrate the company's commitment to sustainability.

The Future of Governance in Sustainable Agriculture

As the agricultural sector continues to evolve, the importance of transparent and ethical governance will only increase. Companies that prioritize transparency, ethical management, risk management, stakeholder engagement, innovation, and ESG reporting will be better positioned to navigate the complex challenges and opportunities of sustainable agriculture.

By building a strong governance framework, agricultural enterprises can enhance their reputation, build trust with stakeholders, and create long-term value. This will not only contribute to the sustainability of their operations but also support the broader goal of creating a more sustainable and resilient food system.

In conclusion, governance is a critical component of sustainable agriculture, providing the foundation for transparent, ethical, and effective management. By prioritizing governance, companies can drive positive change and contribute to a more sustainable future for all.

Conclusion: Integrating ESG into Agriculture for a Sustainable Future

In this chapter, we have seen the significance of ESG—Environmental, Social, and Governance—within the agricultural sector. By understanding and implementing ESG principles, the industry can not only mitigate its environmental impact but also contribute to a more equitable and transparent world.

Reducing the carbon footprint and conserving biodiversity are crucial steps toward sustaining our planet. Equally important is the commitment to social responsibility, which ensures fair labour practices and fosters community engagement. Governance, the third pillar, emphasizes the necessity for transparent and ethical management practices within agricultural enterprises.

Key Takeaways - Key takeaways include the need for actionable strategies to minimize environmental damage, such as adopting sustainable farming techniques and innovative technology. Socially, it is imperative to prioritize the welfare of workers and the surrounding communities by upholding fair labour standards and actively participating in local development. Governance requires a steadfast dedication to transparency, ethical behaviour, and accountability to build trust and long-term success.

Actionable Advice - readers should consider conducting regular ESG audits to identify areas of improvement and develop comprehensive sustainability plans. Engaging stakeholders—from employees to local communities and investors—in ESG initiatives can also drive meaningful and lasting change.

By integrating these principles into their operations, agricultural enterprises can pave the way for a more sustainable and responsible future.

3 INVESTMENT OPPORTUNITIES AND CHALLENGES IN SUSTAINABLE AGRICULTURE

Photo by Gaetano Cessati on Unsplash

In the intricate tapestry of modern agriculture, few threads are as vibrant and promising as those representing sustainable practices. Chapter 3, 'Investment Opportunities and Challenges in Sustainable Agriculture,' invites you on an enlightening journey through the financial landscapes that are reshaping the sector. As the world grapples with the pressing need for environmental stewardship and sustainable development, the intersection of agriculture and investment has emerged as a fertile ground for innovation and growth.

Sustainable agriculture is no longer a just a cool niche or topic for after-dinner conversation - it is a burgeoning field ripe with potential for savvy investors. This chapter begins by identifying high-potential investment areas within sustainable agriculture. From organic farming to regenerative agriculture, from precision farming technologies to vertical farming, the opportunities are as diverse as they are promising. We will delve into the nuances of these investment avenues, offering insights into why they stand out in the crowded marketplace of agricultural innovation.

However, with great opportunity comes great responsibility. Investing in sustainable agriculture necessitates a keen understanding of risk assessment and management. This chapter will guide you through the complexities of evaluating and mitigating risks associated with agricultural investments. Whether it's market volatility, climatic uncertainties, or regulatory changes, understanding these factors is crucial for making informed investment decisions. We will explore strategies employed by seasoned investors to navigate these challenges and protect their investments while contributing to a sustainable future.

The role of policy and regulatory frameworks cannot be understated in shaping the investment landscape of sustainable agriculture. This chapter provides a comprehensive overview of how policies at local, national, and international levels influence investment decisions. From subsidies and grants to regulations and trade policies, the interplay between government actions and private investment is a critical factor in the growth of sustainable agriculture. We will examine case studies and real-world examples to illustrate how policy environments can either foster or hinder investment activities.

Success stories of investors who have reaped the benefits of sustainable agricultural investments serve as powerful testimonials to the potential of this sector. This chapter will highlight several inspiring examples, showcasing how strategic investments have not only yielded significant financial returns but also driven positive environmental and social impacts. These stories will offer valuable lessons and practical insights for new and aspiring investors, demonstrating the tangible benefits of aligning financial goals with sustainability objectives.

As we worth through this section it becomes evident that this field is not merely about capitalizing on market trends. It is about aligning investments with a broader vision of sustainability, resilience, and ethical stewardship of our natural resources. Whether you are an investor looking for lucrative opportunities, a policymaker seeking to understand the investment landscape, or an entrepreneur aiming to innovate within the sector, this chapter provides the knowledge and strategies necessary to navigate the dynamic and rewarding world of sustainable agricultural investments.

Join us as we explore the financial frontier of a greener future, where every investment contributes to a sustainable harvest and a thriving planet.

3.1 Identifying High-Potential Investment Areas within Sustainable Agriculture

In the ever-evolving landscape of sustainable agriculture, identifying high-potential investment areas is crucial for maximizing returns while fostering environmental stewardship. Investors, policymakers, and entrepreneurs are increasingly recognizing the importance of aligning their portfolios with sustainable practices that promise long-term viability and resilience. This section delves into various high-potential investment areas within sustainable agriculture, offering a comprehensive guide to those poised to capitalize on this burgeoning field.

Organic Farming - A Growing Market

Organic farming represents one of the most lucrative and expanding sectors within sustainable agriculture. The global organic food market has experienced consistent growth, driven by increasing consumer demand for healthier, chemical-free food options. Investing in organic farming offers numerous benefits, including access to premium markets and higher profit margins.

Market Dynamics and Trends

The organic farming sector is characterized by several key trends:

- Consumer Awareness: There is a growing awareness among consumers about the health and environmental benefits of organic products. This shift in consumer preference is driving demand and creating opportunities for investors.
- Policy Support: Governments worldwide are implementing policies and incentives to promote organic farming. These include subsidies, tax breaks, and grants aimed at encouraging farmers to adopt organic practices.
- Supply Chain Innovations: Advances in supply chain management, including blockchain technology, are enhancing the traceability and authenticity of organic products, thereby boosting consumer confidence and market growth.

Investment Strategies

To capitalize on the organic farming market, investors should consider the following strategies:

- Direct Investment in Organic Farms: Investing directly in organic farms allows investors to participate in the production process and benefit from higher margins associated with organic products.
- Investment in Supply Chain Infrastructure: Enhancing supply chain infrastructure, such as cold storage facilities and distribution networks, can improve the efficiency and reach of organic products, thereby increasing profitability.
- Supporting Organic Certification Bodies: Investing in organizations that provide organic certification can help ensure the credibility and growth of the organic market.
- Precision Agriculture: Enhancing efficiency and sustainability, precision agriculture leverages advanced technologies, such as GPS, IoT, and data analytics, to optimize farming practices. This approach enhances efficiency, reduces resource wastage, and improves crop yields, making it a high-return investment in this area.

Technological Advancements

The precision agriculture sector is driven by continuous technological advancements, often arising from other sectors:

- Drones and Satellite Imagery: These technologies provide real-time data on crop health, soil conditions, and weather patterns, enabling farmers to make informed decisions.
- IoT Sensors: Internet of Things (IoT) sensors monitor various parameters, including soil moisture, nutrient levels, and temperature, allowing for precise management of resources.
- Data Analytics and AI: Advanced data analytics and artificial intelligence (AI) tools help farmers analyze vast amounts of data to optimize planting schedules, irrigation, and fertilization.

Investment Opportunities

Investors can explore the following opportunities within precision agriculture:

- Technology Providers: Invest in companies that develop and supply precision agriculture technologies, such as drones, sensors, and data analytics platforms.
- Agri-Tech Startups: Supporting innovative startups that are pioneering new precision agriculture solutions.
- Agri-Fintech Integration: Investing in platforms that integrate

financial services with precision agriculture, enabling farmers to access credit and insurance based on data-driven insights and smart contracts on the blockchain.

Aquaculture: Sustainable Seafood Production

Aquaculture, the farming of fish and other aquatic organisms, is emerging as a sustainable solution to meet the growing global demand for seafood. With wild fish stocks under pressure, aquaculture offers a viable alternative that can be managed sustainably.

Sustainable Practices
Sustainable aquaculture practices focus on minimizing environmental impact and ensuring the welfare of aquatic species:

- Closed-Loop Systems: These systems recycle water and waste, reducing pollution and resource consumption.
- Integrated Multi-Trophic Aquaculture (IMTA): This approach involves cultivating multiple species together in a balanced ecosystem, enhancing productivity and sustainability.
- Selective Breeding: Developing strains of fish that are more resilient and require fewer resources.

Investment Potential
The aquaculture sector presents several high-potential investment opportunities:

- Aquaculture Technology: Investing in technologies that enhance the efficiency and sustainability of aquaculture operations, such as automated feeding systems and water quality monitoring.
- Alternative Feed Sources: Supporting the development of sustainable feed sources, such as insect-based or plant-based feeds, to reduce reliance on wild fish stocks.
- Vertical Integration: Investing in vertically integrated aquaculture companies that manage the entire supply chain, from breeding to processing and distribution.

Vertical Farming: Urban Agriculture Revolution

Vertical farming involves growing crops in stacked layers, often in controlled indoor environments. This innovative approach to agriculture addresses the challenges of limited arable land and urbanization, making it a promising investment area.

Benefits and Innovation
Vertical farming offers several benefits and innovations:

- Space Efficiency: Vertical farms maximize the use of space, allowing for high-density crop production in urban areas.
- Controlled Environment Agriculture (CEA): By controlling environmental factors such as light, temperature, and humidity, vertical farms can produce crops year-round, regardless of external weather conditions.
- Resource Efficiency: Vertical farming systems use significantly less water and land compared to traditional farming methods.

Investment Insights
Investors looking to capitalize on vertical farming should consider the following areas:

- Technology Development: Investing in companies that develop advanced vertical farming technologies, such as LED lighting, hydroponic systems, and automation.
- Urban Farming Projects: Supporting urban farming initiatives that bring fresh, locally grown produce to city dwellers.
- Partnerships with Retailers: Collaborating with grocery stores and restaurants to create a direct supply chain for vertically farmed produce.

Regenerative Agriculture: Restoring Ecosystems
Regenerative agriculture goes beyond sustainability by actively restoring and enhancing ecosystems. This approach focuses on improving soil health, increasing biodiversity, and sequestering carbon, making it a compelling investment area for those committed to environmental impact.

The core principles of regenerative agriculture include:

- Soil Health: Practices such as cover cropping, crop rotation, and reduced tillage improve soil structure and fertility.
- Biodiversity: Incorporating a diverse range of plant and animal species enhances ecosystem resilience and productivity.
- Carbon Sequestration: Regenerative practices capture atmospheric

carbon and store it in the soil, mitigating climate change.

Investment Pathways
Investors can explore several pathways within regenerative agriculture:

- Land Restoration Projects: Investing in projects that restore degraded lands through regenerative practices.
- Regenerative Product Lines: Supporting companies that produce, and market products derived from regenerative agriculture.
- Ecosystem Services Markets: Participating in emerging markets for ecosystem services, such as carbon credits and biodiversity offsets, generated by regenerative farming practices.

Conclusion - Strategic Considerations
Investors looking to get involved in sustainable agriculture require a strategic approach that aligns their financial goals with environmental and social impacts.

By identifying high-return areas, investors can contribute to the transformation of the agriculture sector while achieving significant returns.

Key considerations include:

- Due Diligence: Conduct thorough due diligence to assess the sustainability and profitability of potential investments.
- Long-Term Perspective: Adopt a long-term perspective, recognizing that sustainable agriculture investments may take time to realize their full potential.
- Collaboration: Engage with stakeholders, including farmers, policymakers, and technology providers, to create synergies and drive innovation.

By focusing on high-ROI (Return on Investment) areas such as organic farming, precision agriculture, aquaculture, vertical farming, and regenerative agriculture, investors can play a pivotal role in advancing sustainable agriculture and securing a resilient future for our food systems.

3.2 Navigating the Terrain: Risk & Agricultural Investments

Investing in agriculture, like any other sector, comes with its own set of risks. However, the unique nature of agriculture - being heavily influenced by environmental factors, market fluctuations, and global economic conditions makes risk assessment and management particularly challenging.

Understanding these risks is crucial for investors, policymakers, and entrepreneurs who aim to make sustainable and profitable investments in this sector.

Types of Risks in Agricultural Investments

1. Climate and Weather-related Risks: Agriculture is fundamentally dependent on climatic conditions. Changes in rainfall patterns, temperature fluctuations, and extreme weather events such as droughts, floods, and hurricanes can significantly affect crop yields and livestock productivity. These climate-related risks are further exacerbated by the ongoing impacts of climate change, which introduce greater uncertainty and variability into agricultural production.
2. Market and Price Risks: Agricultural markets are highly volatile. Prices of agricultural commodities can fluctuate widely due to factors such as supply-demand imbalances, trade policies, and global economic conditions. For instance, a surplus in production can lead to a sharp decline in prices, adversely affecting farmers' income and investors' returns. Conversely, a shortage can drive prices up, raising concerns about food security and affordability across society.
3. Biological and Environmental Risks: Agricultural production is susceptible to various biological risks, including pests, diseases, and invasive species. These can devastate crops and livestock, leading to significant economic losses. Additionally, environmental factors such as soil degradation, water scarcity, and loss of biodiversity pose long-term risks to the sustainability of agricultural practices.
4. Regulatory and Policy Risks: Agricultural investments are also influenced by government policies and regulations. Changes in agricultural subsidies, trade agreements, and environmental regulations can create uncertainties for investors. For example, the introduction of stricter environmental standards may increase production costs, while changes in trade policies can affect market access and competitiveness.
5. Operational and Management Risks: Operational risks arise from the day-to-day management of agricultural enterprises. This can include risks related to labour, productivity, supply chain disruptions, and technological failures. Effective management practices and the adoption of advanced technologies can mitigate some of these risks, but they require significant

investment and expertise.

Risk Assessment Strategies

To effectively manage risks in agricultural investments, it is essential to conduct thorough risk assessments. This involves identifying potential risks, evaluating their likelihood and impact, and developing mitigation strategies.

1. Risk Identification: The first step in risk assessment is to identify the various risks that may affect the investment. This requires a sound understanding of the agricultural sector, including the specific crops or livestock involved, the geographical area, and the broader economic and environmental context. Tools such as SWOT analysis (Strengths, Weaknesses, Opportunities, and Threats) can be useful in this process.
2. Risk Evaluation: Once the risks have been identified, the next step is to evaluate their likelihood and potential impact. This involves both qualitative and quantitative analysis. Qualitative analysis may include expert opinions and scenario planning, while quantitative analysis can involve statistical modelling and financial metrics such as Value at Risk (VaR) and Expected Shortfall (ES).
3. Risk Mitigation: After evaluating the risks, it is crucial to develop strategies to mitigate them. This can involve a combination of techniques, including diversification, insurance, and the adoption of sustainable practices.

Risk Management Techniques

1. Diversification: One of the most effective ways to manage risk in agricultural investments is through diversification. This can involve diversifying across different crops and livestock, geographical regions, and stages of the value chain. For example, investing in both crop production and food processing can reduce exposure to risks associated with any single segment of the agricultural sector.
2. Insurance: Agricultural insurance is another critical tool for managing risk. Crop insurance, for instance, can provide financial compensation for losses due to adverse weather conditions, pests, and diseases. Livestock insurance can cover risks such as disease outbreaks and mortality. Moreover, parametric insurance, which pays out based on predefined indices (e.g., rainfall levels), offers a more straightforward and quicker claims process.
3. Sustainable Practices: Adopting sustainable agricultural practices can also help mitigate risks. Practices such as crop rotation, integrated pest

management, and conservation tillage can enhance soil health, reduce pest and disease incidence, and improve resilience to climate variability. Furthermore, sustainable practices can reduce reliance on external inputs such as chemical fertilizers and pesticides, thereby lowering production costs and environmental impacts.

4. Technological Innovations: Technological advancements play a crucial role in risk management. Precision agriculture technologies, such as remote sensing, GPS-guided machinery, and data analytics, enable farmers to optimize resource use, monitor crop health, and make data-driven decisions. Biotechnological innovations, such as genetically modified crops and advanced breeding techniques, can enhance resistance to pests, diseases, and environmental stresses.

Case Studies: Successful Risk Management in Practice

- The Role of Cooperatives in Risk Mitigation

Agricultural cooperatives have proven to be effective in managing risks for small-scale farmers. By pooling resources and sharing risks, cooperatives can provide their members with access to better inputs, credit, and markets. For instance, the Fairtrade movement has supported cooperatives in developing countries, enabling them to achieve higher and more stable incomes through access to premium markets and fair pricing.

- Public-Private Partnerships for Risk Management

Public-private partnerships (PPPs) can also play a significant role in risk management. By combining the strengths of public institutions and private enterprises, PPPs can facilitate access to advanced technologies, infrastructure, and financial services. One example might be the African Risk Capacity (ARC), a specialized agency of the African Union that provides insurance and risk management solutions to African countries vulnerable to climate-related disasters. "ARC's mission is to use modern finance mechanisms, such as risk pooling and risk transfer, to create pan-African climate response systems that enable African countries to meet the needs of people vulnerable to natural disasters."

- Innovative Financial Instruments

Innovative financial instruments, such as green bonds and impact investing, offer new avenues for managing risks in agricultural investments. Green bonds, for example, can finance projects that promote sustainable agricultural practices, thereby reducing environmental risks. Impact investing focuses on generating social and environmental benefits alongside financial returns, aligning with the principles of ESG.

The Role of Policy in Risk Management

Effective risk management in agricultural investments also requires supportive policies and regulatory frameworks. Governments can play a crucial role in creating an enabling environment for sustainable agriculture through policies that promote research and development, infrastructure development, and market access.

1. Research and Development - Investment in agricultural research and development (R&D) is essential for developing new technologies and practices that enhance overall resilience. Governments can support R&D through funding, partnerships with academic institutions, and incentives for private sector involvement.
2. Infrastructure Development - Adequate infrastructure is vital for mitigating risks related to transportation, storage, and market access. Governments can invest in rural infrastructure, such as roads, irrigation systems, and storage facilities, to reduce post-harvest losses and improve market connectivity.
3. Market Access and Trade Policies - Policies that promote market access and fair trade can help to stabilize agricultural markets and reduce price volatility. This includes trade agreements, export incentives, and mechanisms for price stabilization. Additionally, policies that support the establishment of farmers' markets and cooperatives can enhance market access for small-scale producers.

Conclusion: A Holistic Approach to Risk Management

In conclusion, effective risk management in agricultural investments requires a holistic approach that integrates various strategies and stakeholders. By understanding the diverse risks involved and implementing robust risk assessment and management techniques, investors, policymakers, and entrepreneurs can navigate the complexities of the agricultural sector and achieve sustainable and profitable outcomes.

The journey towards a sustainable harvest is fraught with challenges but with careful planning and a strategic approach, it is possible to secure a future where agriculture thrives in harmony with our planet.

3.3 How Policy and Regulation Shapes Sustainable Agriculture

The intersection of sustainable agriculture and investment is a fertile ground for potential growth, innovation, and environmental stewardship. However, the journey to realize these opportunities is highly contingent upon the policy and regulatory frameworks that govern the agriculture sector. These frameworks play a pivotal role in shaping investment trajectories, ensuring that financial flows align with sustainable practices, and mitigating risks associated with agricultural investments. This section delves deep into the intricate relationship between policy, regulation, and investment in sustainable agriculture, providing a comprehensive understanding of how these elements coalesce to drive impactful change.

The Foundation of Policy and Regulatory Frameworks
Policy and regulatory frameworks in agriculture have evolved significantly over the past century. Initially, the focus was predominantly on food security and agricultural productivity, with little regard for environmental sustainability or social equity. However, growing awareness of climate change, biodiversity loss, and social inequalities has prompted a paradigm shift towards more holistic and sustainable approaches. This evolution is reflected in contemporary policies that integrate Environmental, Social, and Governance (ESG) principles, aiming to create a more balanced and resilient agricultural sector.

Key Policy Instruments and Mechanisms
Several policy instruments and mechanisms are instrumental in shaping sustainable agriculture investments. These include subsidies, tax incentives, grants, and regulatory standards. Subsidies and tax incentives can lower the financial barriers for investors, making sustainable agriculture more attractive. Grants can provide the necessary capital for innovative projects, while regulatory standards ensure that agricultural practices meet specific environmental and social criteria. Together, these instruments create a conducive environment for sustainable investments, fostering a culture of innovation and responsibility.

Aligning Investments with ESG Principles
Environmental policies are critical in steering investments towards sustainable

agriculture. Regulations on pesticide use, water management, and soil conservation ensure that agricultural practices do not compromise the environment. Policies promoting organic farming, agroforestry, and regenerative agriculture further incentivize sustainable practices. For investors, these policies reduce environmental risks and enhance the long-term viability of their investments. By aligning financial flows with environmental sustainability, these policies help create a resilient agricultural sector that can withstand the challenges posed by climate change and resource depletion.

Social Policies and Community Engagement
Social policies play a crucial role in ensuring that agricultural investments benefit local communities and promote social equity. Policies aimed at improving labour conditions, ensuring fair wages, and protecting the rights of smallholder farmers are essential components of a sustainable agricultural framework. Community engagement initiatives, supported by policy frameworks, can foster inclusive growth and ensure that investments contribute to the well-being of all stakeholders. For investors, these policies mitigate social risks and enhance the social license to operate, creating a positive impact on both the community and the investment portfolio.

Governance Policies and Transparency
Good governance is a cornerstone of sustainable agriculture investments. Policies promoting transparency, accountability, and ethical practices are vital in building investor confidence and ensuring the integrity of agricultural projects. Governance policies that mandate disclosure of ESG performance, regular audits, and stakeholder consultations can enhance the credibility and attractiveness of sustainable agriculture investments. For policymakers, creating a robust governance framework is essential in fostering a transparent and accountable agricultural sector that aligns with broader ESG goals.

Navigating Regulatory Challenges
Regulatory Barriers and Solutions
While policy frameworks can facilitate sustainable agriculture investments, regulatory barriers can pose significant challenges. Complex and inconsistent regulations, bureaucratic red tape, and lack of clarity can deter investors and hinder the adoption of sustainable practices.

To overcome these challenges, policymakers must streamline regulatory processes, harmonize standards, and provide clear guidelines for investors. Collaborative platforms involving regulators, investors, and agricultural stakeholders can also help address regulatory bottlenecks and create a more enabling environment for sustainable investments.

Regulatory Success and Failure
Examining case studies of regulatory success and failure provides valuable insights into the role of policy frameworks in shaping sustainable agriculture investments. For instance, the European Union's Common Agricultural Policy (CAP) has been instrumental in promoting sustainable practices through subsidies and environmental standards.

Conversely, the lack of coherent policies in some developing countries has hindered sustainable agriculture investments, highlighting the need for comprehensive and context-specific regulatory frameworks.

These two cases underscore the importance of effective policy design and implementation in driving sustainable agricultural outcomes.

The Role of International Agreements and Collaborations

Global Initiatives and Frameworks
International agreements and collaborations play a vital role in shaping national and regional policies for sustainable agriculture. Agreements such as the Paris Climate Accord, the Sustainable Development Goals (SDGs), and the Convention on Biological Diversity (CBD) provide a global framework for aligning agricultural practices with environmental and social objectives. These international commitments create a shared vision and set common standards, encouraging countries to adopt policies that support sustainable agriculture. For investors, these global frameworks offer a level of predictability and assurance, fostering cross-border investments in sustainable agricultural projects.

Regional Collaborations and Trade Agreements
Regional collaborations and trade agreements can further enhance the policy environment for sustainable agriculture investments. Regional bodies such as the European Union, the African Union, and ASEAN have developed policies and initiatives to promote sustainable agriculture within their regions. Trade agreements that include provisions for environmental protection and social equity can also drive sustainable practices. For investors, regional collaborations and trade agreements can open up new markets and create opportunities for scaling sustainable agricultural projects, enhancing the overall impact and profitability of their investments.

Future Directions and Policy Recommendations

Emerging Trends and Innovations

The future of sustainable agriculture is being shaped by emerging trends and innovations in policy and regulation. Policies promoting digital agriculture, precision farming, and climate-smart practices are gaining traction, offering new avenues for sustainable investments.

Innovations in policy design, such as outcome-based incentives and public-private partnerships, are also creating more dynamic and responsive regulatory frameworks.

For investors, staying abreast of these trends and understanding their implications is crucial for identifying and capitalizing on emerging opportunities in sustainable agriculture.

Strategic Policy Recommendations

To foster a more conducive environment for sustainable agriculture investments, policymakers must adopt strategic approaches that integrate ESG principles. Key recommendations include:

1. Enhancing Policy Coherence: Ensuring that environmental, social, and economic policies are aligned and mutually reinforcing.
2. Strengthening Institutional Capacity: Building the capacity of regulatory bodies to effectively implement and enforce policies.
3. Promoting Multi-Stakeholder Collaboration: Encouraging collaboration between government, private sector, and civil society to create inclusive and participatory policy processes.
4. Supporting Innovation and Research: Investing in research and development to drive innovation in sustainable agriculture practices and technologies.
5. Ensuring Long-Term Policy Stability: Providing a stable and predictable policy environment to build investor confidence and encourage long-term investments.

By adopting these strategic recommendations, policymakers can create a robust and supportive policy framework that drives sustainable agriculture investments, contributing to a greener and more resilient future.

Conclusion

Policy and regulatory frameworks are the bedrock of sustainable agriculture investments. They provide the necessary guidance, incentives, and safeguards to ensure that financial flows align with environmental, social, and governance objectives. By understanding the intricate interplay between policy, regulation, and investment, stakeholders can navigate the complexities of sustainable agriculture and unlock its full potential.

As we move towards a more sustainable future, the role of policy and regulatory frameworks will be paramount in shaping a resilient and thriving agricultural sector that benefits people, planet, and profit alike.

3.4 Success Stories of Investors in Sustainable Agriculture

In the rapidly evolving landscape of sustainable agriculture, several visionary investors have emerged over the years as frontrunners, sowing the seeds of innovation and reaping remarkable returns. These success stories serve not only as a testament to the viability of sustainable practices but also as a beacon for other investors seeking to make a meaningful impact while achieving financial growth.

In this section, we look into a few of the inspiring journeys of some of the most successful investors in sustainable agriculture, exploring their strategies, challenges, and the transformative outcomes of their ventures.

The Regenerative Revolution - Indigo Agriculture

Indigo Agriculture stands as both a prime example and an investment warning as to how innovative thinking can drive sustainable practices while generating significant returns. Founded in 2013, Indigo Agriculture focuses on harnessing the power of nature to help farmers sustainably feed the planet. The company uses microbiology and digital technologies to improve crop resilience and productivity, thereby reducing the environmental footprint of agriculture.

Investment Strategy and Impact
Indigo Agriculture attracted early investments from prominent venture capital firms like Flagship Pioneering. The company's approach to regenerative agriculture—emphasizing soil health, carbon sequestration, and biodiversity—resonated with investors looking for sustainable solutions. By 2020, Indigo had raised over $1.2 billion in funding, showcasing the strong investor confidence in its mission.

Transformative Outcomes

Indigo's impact has been multifaceted. Their innovative microbial seed coatings have increased crop yields while reducing the need for chemical fertilizers and pesticides. Additionally, Indigo's carbon marketplace initiative enables farmers to earn revenue by adopting regenerative practices that sequester carbon in the soil. This dual benefit of enhancing farm profitability and addressing climate change has positioned Indigo as a leader in the sustainable agriculture sector.

The Power of Partnerships - Farmland LP

Farmland LP is another compelling success story, illustrating the potential of sustainable agriculture to attract diverse investments and generate impressive returns. Founded in 2009, Farmland LP acquires conventional farmland and transitions it to organic, sustainably managed operations. The company emphasizes the ecological and financial benefits of sustainable farming practices.

Investment Strategy and Impact

Farmland LP's innovative model has attracted a mix of private and institutional investors. By focusing on long-term land appreciation and sustainable farm management, Farmland LP has delivered consistent returns. The company's investment strategy includes leveraging partnerships with organic certification bodies, research institutions, and sustainable farming organizations to enhance farm productivity and profitability.

Transformative Outcomes

The transition of conventional farmland to organic management has yielded significant benefits. Farmland LP's properties have experienced increased biodiversity, improved soil health, and higher crop yields. Financially, the company has achieved an average annual return of over 8%, demonstrating the economic viability of sustainable farming practices. Farmland LP's success has inspired other investors to consider sustainable agriculture as a lucrative and impactful investment avenue.

The Power of Vertical - AeroFarms

AeroFarms represents a groundbreaking success in the realm of vertical farming and sustainable agriculture. Founded in 2004, AeroFarms utilizes aeroponic technology to grow crops in controlled indoor environments, significantly reducing water usage and eliminating the need for pesticides.

Investment Strategy and Impact
AeroFarms has attracted substantial investment from venture capital firms, government grants, and strategic partnerships. By 2021, the company had raised over $238 million in funding. AeroFarms' investors were drawn to the company's innovative approach to addressing food security and sustainability challenges.

Transformative Outcomes
AeroFarms' is one high-flying agritech company with a technology-driven approach, vertical farming, that has led to remarkable outcomes. The company's vertical farms use 95% less water than traditional farming methods and produce yields up to 390 times higher per square foot.

AeroFarms has also expanded its reach, supplying fresh produce to major retailers and food service providers. The company's success has paved the way for the broader adoption of vertical farming as a sustainable solution to urban and global food challenges.

The Global Impact - Rabobank's Food & Agribusiness Fund
Rabobank, a global leader in food and agribusiness banking, has demonstrated the power of strategic investment in sustainable agriculture through its Food & Agribusiness Fund. This fund focuses on financing innovative projects and companies that promote sustainable food production and supply chain practices.

Investment Strategy and Impact
Rabobank's fund leverages the bank's extensive industry expertise and global network to identify high-potential investment opportunities. By providing capital and advisory services, Rabobank supports companies that drive sustainability and innovation in agriculture.

The fund's investment strategy includes a strong emphasis on ESG criteria, ensuring that investments contribute to environmental and social well-being.

Transformative Outcomes
Rabobank's investments have led to significant advancements in sustainable agriculture. Companies funded by Rabobank have developed groundbreaking technologies, such as precision farming tools, sustainable packaging solutions, and alternative protein sources. These innovations have not only enhanced the sustainability of food production but also created new market opportunities and consumer products. Rabobank's success underscores the

importance of strategic investment in fostering a sustainable and resilient food system.

Lessons Learned: Key Takeaways for Investors

The success stories of Indigo Agriculture, Farmland LP, AeroFarms, and Rabobank's Food & Agribusiness Fund offer valuable insights for investors seeking to engage in sustainable agriculture. Here are some key takeaways:

1. Embrace Innovation and Technology - Investing in companies that leverage cutting-edge technologies and innovative practices can yield substantial returns while driving sustainability. From microbial seed treatments to vertical farming, technological advancements play a crucial role in transforming agriculture.
2. Focus on Long-Term Impact - Sustainable agriculture investments often require a long-term perspective. Investors should be prepared to support companies through the transition to sustainable practices and recognize the enduring benefits of improved soil health, biodiversity, and climate resilience.
3. Leverage Partnerships and Networks - Collaborating with industry experts, research institutions, and sustainable farming organizations can enhance the success of sustainable agriculture investments. These partnerships provide valuable resources, knowledge, and market access.
4. Prioritize ESG Criteria - Incorporating Environmental, Social, and Governance (ESG) criteria into investment decisions ensures that investments align with broader sustainability goals. This approach not only mitigates risks but also enhances the positive impact of investments.
5. Recognize the Market Potential - The growing consumer demand for sustainable and organic products presents significant market opportunities. Investors can capitalize on this trend by supporting companies that prioritize sustainability and cater to eco-conscious consumers.

Planting the Seeds for a Sustainable Future

The success stories highlighted in this section demonstrate the transformative potential of sustainable agriculture investments. By embracing innovation, focusing on long-term impact, leveraging partnerships, prioritizing ESG criteria, and recognizing market potential, investors can drive meaningful change while achieving financial success. As the global community seeks to address the pressing challenges of food security, climate change, and environmental degradation, sustainable agriculture offers a promising path forward. These inspiring examples serve as a call to action for investors to join the movement towards a sustainable harvest and contribute to a resilient and

Conclusion

As we conclude Chapter 3, it becomes evident that sustainable agriculture offers a plethora of high-potential investment opportunities that are not only financially rewarding but also environmentally and socially responsible. By identifying key areas such as organic farming, regenerative agriculture, and agri-tech innovations, investors can tap into a growing market driven by increasing consumer demand for sustainable products.

However, it is crucial to approach these investments with a comprehensive risk assessment and management strategy. Factors such as climate change, market volatility, and supply chain disruptions must be meticulously evaluated to mitigate potential risks. Additionally, understanding the role of policy and regulatory frameworks is essential for navigating the complexities of agricultural investments. Governments and international bodies are increasingly supporting sustainable practices through incentives and regulations, which can significantly impact investment outcomes.

The success stories highlighted in this chapter demonstrate that with the right strategy, sustainable agriculture can yield substantial returns. These case studies underscore the importance of thorough research, strategic partnerships, and a long-term vision. As an actionable takeaway, investors are encouraged to stay informed about emerging trends, engage with policy developments, and collaborate with industry experts to maximize their impact and profitability in the realm of sustainable agriculture.

Ultimately, the intersection of agriculture and ESG principles offers a transformative avenue for investment, fostering a future where economic growth harmonizes with environmental stewardship and social responsibility.

4 INNOVATIONS AND TECHNOLOGIES SHAPING THE FUTURE

Source Pexels - Photo by Anton Klyuchnikov

In the ever-evolving agricultural landscape, the integration of cutting-edge technologies is not just a trend but a necessity. As the global population continues to surge and climate change imposes unprecedented challenges, the need for more efficient, resilient, and sustainable agricultural practices has never been more pressing.

Chapter 4 of 'Green From Green III - Sustainable Harvest - The Intersection of Agriculture and ESG' discusses into some of the groundbreaking innovations and technologies that are revolutionizing the agricultural sector, offering new avenues for growth, sustainability, and profitability.

One of the most transformative advancements in recent years is the advent of precision farming. Utilizing tools such as drones, sensors, and satellite imagery, precision farming allows for real-time monitoring and management of crops, leading to optimized resource usage and enhanced yield outcomes. This technology not only minimizes waste but also ensures that every hectare of farmland reaches its maximum potential. Precision farming stands as a beacon of efficiency in an industry that is often at the mercy of unpredictable environmental factors.

Alongside precision farming, the Internet of Things (IoT) and Artificial Intelligence (AI) are ushering in a new era of smart agriculture. IoT devices collect vast amounts of data from the field, which AI algorithms then analyse to provide actionable insights. These insights enable farmers to make informed decisions regarding irrigation, pest control, and crop rotation, thereby reducing costs and improving productivity. The fusion of IoT and AI is creating a more connected and intelligent agricultural ecosystem, where data-driven decisions lead to sustainable practices and robust food security.

As we turn our attention to aquaculture, the blue economy is witnessing its own wave of innovation. Sustainable aquaculture practices are crucial for maintaining the health of our oceans while meeting the growing demand for seafood. Technological advancements such as automated feeding systems, water quality monitoring, and genetic selection are enhancing the efficiency and sustainability of aquaculture operations. These innovations not only boost production but also ensure that aquaculture practices are environmentally responsible and economically viable.

Renewable energy solutions are also playing a pivotal role in transforming agriculture and aquaculture. The adoption of solar panels, wind turbines, hybrid off-grid power systems and bioenergy systems are all reducing the sector's reliance on fossil fuels and lowering their carbon footprint. Renewable energy not only provides a sustainable power source but also offers cost savings and energy security for agricultural operations. By harnessing the power of nature, farmers and aquaculturists can create more resilient and sustainable production systems.

Blockchain technology is becoming another game-changer in the agricultural landscape. By providing transparency and traceability in the food supply chain, blockchain ensures that every step from farm to table is documented and verifiable. This transparency builds trust among consumers, enhances food safety, and reduces the risk of fraud. Moreover, blockchain can streamline supply chain operations, reduce inefficiencies, and create new opportunities for value-added services. In a world where consumers are increasingly demanding to know the origins of their food, the blockchain offers a robust solution for ensuring integrity and accountability.

As we explore these innovations and technologies, it becomes evident that the future of agriculture is not just about growing more food but growing it smarter and more sustainably. The integration of precision farming, IoT, AI, renewable energy, and blockchain is setting the stage for a new agricultural era, one that aligns with ESG principles and paves the way for a greener, more resilient food system. Chapter 4 provides an overview of these cutting-edge technologies, offering valuable insights and practical strategies for policymakers, investors, and entrepreneurs who are committed to driving impactful change in the agricultural sector. Join us as we embark on this exciting journey into the future of sustainable agriculture, where innovation meets responsibility and technology becomes the cornerstone of a thriving, sustainable harvest.

4.1 The Technological Renaissance: Precision Farming, IoT, and AI in Agriculture

In the 21st century, agriculture is experiencing a technological renaissance, driven by groundbreaking innovations that promise to revolutionize food production, enhance sustainability, and ensure food security for the growing global population. At the heart of this transformation are precision farming, the Internet of Things (IoT), and Artificial Intelligence (AI). These cutting-edge technologies are not just buzzwords; they are vital tools that are reshaping the agricultural landscape and paving the way for a more efficient and sustainable future.

Precision Farming - The Art of Data-Driven Agriculture

Precision farming, also known as precision agriculture, is an innovative farming management concept that uses information technology to ensure that crops and soil receive exactly what they need for optimal health and productivity. This approach relies on data analytics and a variety of technologies, including GPS mapping, remote sensing, and variable rate technology (VRT), to monitor and manage agricultural practices with unprecedented accuracy.

GPS Mapping and Remote Sensing
GPS mapping and remote sensing are at the core of precision farming. GPS technology allows farmers to create detailed maps of their fields, providing critical data on soil types, nutrient levels, and crop conditions. This information is essential for making informed decisions about planting, fertilizing, and harvesting.

Remote sensing, often conducted using drones or satellites, offers real-time data on crop health, moisture levels, and pest infestations. These tools enable farmers to identify problems early and take corrective actions promptly, thereby minimizing crop losses and maximizing yields.

Variable Rate Technology (VRT)
Variable Rate Technology (VRT) is another crucial component of precision farming. VRT allows farmers to apply inputs such as fertilizers, pesticides, and water at variable rates across a field, or timed based on weather and seasonal condition, rather than uniformly. This targeted approach ensures that each part of the field receives the exact amount of input it needs, optimizing resource use and reducing waste. By tailoring inputs to the specific needs of different areas, VRT not only enhances crop productivity but also promotes environmental sustainability by minimizing the overuse of chemicals and water.

The Benefits of Precision Farming
The advantages of precision farming are manifold.

First and foremost, it leads to higher crop yields and better-quality produce. By providing crops with optimal growing conditions, precision farming maximizes their potential, resulting in more abundant and nutritious harvests.

Additionally, precision farming reduces input costs by minimizing waste and ensuring efficient use of resources. This cost-effectiveness is particularly beneficial for small and medium-sized farms, which often operate on tight budgets.

Moreover, precision farming plays a critical role in environmental conservation. By reducing the overapplication of fertilizers and pesticides, it mitigates the risk of soil degradation, water contamination, and biodiversity loss. This sustainable approach not only safeguards the environment but also enhances the long-term viability of agricultural operations.

Finally, precision farming contributes to food security by increasing the resilience of agricultural systems to climate change and other challenges. By enabling farmers to adapt to changing conditions and optimize their practices, it ensures a stable and reliable food supply for the future.

The Internet of Things (IoT) - Connecting the Farm

The Internet of Things (IoT) is another transformative technology that is revolutionizing agriculture. IoT refers to the network of interconnected devices that communicate and exchange data with each other via the internet. In the context of agriculture, IoT encompasses a wide range of smart devices, sensors, and equipment that collect and transmit data on various aspects of farming operations.

Smart Sensors and Monitoring Systems
Smart sensors are at the forefront of IoT applications in agriculture. These sensors can be placed in fields, greenhouses, and livestock facilities to monitor a variety of parameters, including soil moisture, temperature, humidity, and nutrient levels. The data collected by these sensors is transmitted to central systems, where it can be analysed and used to make informed decisions about irrigation, fertilization, and pest control.

For example, soil moisture sensors can provide real-time data on water levels, allowing farmers to optimize irrigation schedules and avoid overwatering or underwatering their crops.

Livestock Monitoring
IoT technology is also transforming livestock management. Wearable devices and smart collars equipped with sensors can monitor the health and behaviour of animals, providing valuable insights into their well-being. These devices can track vital signs, detect signs of illness, and monitor feeding and movement patterns. By leveraging this data, farmers can ensure that their livestock receive the appropriate care and nutrition, leading to healthier animals and higher-quality produce.

Automated Farm Equipment
IoT-enabled farm equipment, such as tractors, harvesters, and irrigation systems, can operate autonomously or be remotely controlled. These smart machines can perform tasks with precision and efficiency, reducing the need for manual labour and minimizing human error. For instance, autonomous tractors can follow GPS-guided routes to plough fields, plant seeds, and apply inputs with pinpoint accuracy. Similarly, IoT-enabled irrigation systems can adjust water flow based on real-time data from soil moisture sensors, ensuring optimal water usage and reducing waste.

The Impact of IoT on Agriculture
The integration of IoT in agriculture offers numerous benefits. It enhances the efficiency and effectiveness of farming operations by providing real-time data and insights. This data-driven approach enables farmers to make informed decisions, optimize resource use, and improve crop and livestock

management.

Additionally, IoT technology increases the automation of agricultural processes, reducing labour costs and increasing productivity. By streamlining operations and minimizing manual intervention, IoT allows farmers to focus on strategic planning and innovation.

Furthermore, IoT contributes to sustainability by promoting resource conservation and reducing environmental impact. By optimizing water usage, minimizing chemical inputs, and reducing waste, IoT-enabled practices support sustainable farming and environmental stewardship.

Lastly, IoT enhances traceability and transparency in the food supply chain. By tracking and recording data on the production, processing, and distribution of agricultural products, IoT helps ensure food safety, quality, and authenticity, building consumer trust and confidence.

Artificial Intelligence (AI): The Brain Behind Smart Farming

Artificial Intelligence (AI) is the third pillar of the technological renaissance in agriculture. AI encompasses a range of technologies, including machine learning, deep learning, and computer vision, that enable machines to mimic human intelligence and perform complex tasks. In agriculture, AI is being leveraged to analyse data, optimize processes, and provide actionable insights.

Predictive Analytics and Decision Support

One of the most significant applications of AI in agriculture is predictive analytics. By analysing historical data and current conditions, AI algorithms can predict future trends and outcomes, helping farmers make proactive decisions.

For example, AI can forecast weather patterns, pest infestations, and disease outbreaks, allowing farmers to take preventive measures and minimize risks. Decision support systems powered by AI can provide personalized recommendations on planting, fertilizing, and harvesting, based on real-time data and predictive models.

Crop and Soil Health Monitoring

AI-powered systems can analyse data from various sources, including sensors, drones, and satellite imagery, to monitor crop and soil health. Computer vision technology, a subset of AI, can process images and identify signs of stress, disease, or nutrient deficiencies in crops. This early detection enables farmers to address issues promptly and prevent crop losses.

Additionally, AI can analyse soil data to assess fertility, structure, and moisture levels, providing insights into soil health and guiding soil management practices.

Autonomous Farming Equipment
AI is also driving the development of autonomous farming equipment. Self-driving tractors, harvesters, and drones equipped with AI capabilities can perform tasks with precision and efficiency. These autonomous machines can navigate fields, avoid obstacles, and execute complex operations without human intervention. By automating labour-intensive tasks, AI reduces the physical burden on farmers and enhances productivity.

The Impact of AI on Agriculture
The adoption of AI in agriculture offers numerous advantages. It enhances decision-making by providing data-driven insights and predictive analytics. This enables farmers to optimize their practices, reduce risks, and increase yields. AI also improves resource management by identifying inefficiencies and recommending optimal input levels. By minimizing waste and maximizing resource use, AI supports sustainable farming and cost savings.

Moreover, AI boosts productivity and efficiency by automating tasks and streamlining operations. This allows farmers to focus on strategic planning and innovation, rather than manual labour. AI also contributes to food security by enhancing the resilience of agricultural systems. By predicting and mitigating risks, AI ensures a stable and reliable food supply. Finally, AI promotes precision and accuracy in farming practices, leading to higher-quality produce and improved food safety.

Integrating Technologies: The Synergy of Precision Farming, IoT, and AI

The true potential of these cutting-edge technologies lies in their integration. When combined, precision farming, IoT, and AI create a synergistic effect that amplifies their individual benefits and drives transformative change in agriculture. This integrated approach, often referred to as smart farming or digital agriculture, leverages the strengths of each technology to create a holistic and data-driven farming system.

Data Collection and Analysis
The integration of precision farming, IoT, and AI enables comprehensive data

collection and analysis. IoT sensors and devices continuously gather data on various aspects of farming operations, from soil conditions and weather patterns to crop health and livestock behaviour. This data is then analysed by AI algorithms, which provide actionable insights and recommendations. Precision farming tools, such as GPS mapping and VRT, use this data to optimize inputs and practices, ensuring that resources are used efficiently and effectively.

Automation and Efficiency
The synergy of these technologies also enhances automation and efficiency. IoT-enabled equipment and AI-powered systems can perform tasks autonomously, increasing safety for employees and minimizing human error.

Precision farming techniques ensure that these tasks are executed with accuracy and precision, maximizing productivity and minimizing waste. This automation not only increases efficiency but also frees up farmers' own time, allowing them to focus on strategic decision-making and innovation.

Sustainability and Environmental Stewardship
The integrated approach of precision farming, IoT, and AI promotes sustainability and environmental stewardship. By optimizing resource use and reducing waste, these technologies minimize the environmental impact of farming practices.

Precision farming techniques, such as VRT, ensure that inputs are applied only where needed, reducing the risk of soil degradation and water contamination. IoT sensors monitor environmental conditions in real-time, enabling farmers to respond to changes promptly and mitigate negative impacts. AI algorithms analyse data to identify opportunities for further sustainability improvements, guiding farmers towards more eco-friendly practices.

Challenges and Considerations
While the benefits of precision farming, IoT, and AI are undeniable, their adoption comes with challenges and considerations. One of the primary challenges is the high cost of technology and infrastructure. Implementing these advanced systems requires significant investment, which could unfortunately be a barrier for small and medium-sized farms, but these technologies are becoming more accessible all the time.

Additionally, there is a need for technical expertise and training to operate and maintain these technologies effectively. To survive, farmers must be equipped with the skills and knowledge to leverage the full potential of precision farming, IoT, and AI.

Data privacy and security are also critical considerations. The extensive data collection involved in smart farming raises concerns about data ownership, access, and protection. Ensuring that data is securely stored and used ethically is essential to building trust and confidence among farmers and stakeholders. Furthermore, the integration of these technologies requires robust connectivity and infrastructure, particularly in rural and remote areas. Addressing the digital divide and ensuring reliable internet access is crucial for the widespread adoption of smart farming practices and long term sustainability.

The Future of Agriculture - Embracing Innovation
The technological renaissance in agriculture, driven by precision farming, IoT, and AI, promises a more efficient, sustainable, and resilient future. By embracing these cutting-edge technologies, the agricultural sector can overcome challenges, optimise practices, and achieve greater productivity and sustainability. Policymakers, investors, and entrepreneurs play a vital role in supporting the adoption and integration of these technologies, providing the necessary resources, infrastructure, and incentives to drive innovation.

As we look to the future, fostering collaboration and knowledge-sharing within the agricultural community is essential. By working together, farmers, researchers, technology providers, and policymakers can develop and implement solutions that address the unique needs and challenges of the agricultural sector. Embracing a holistic and data-driven approach, we can pave the way for a sustainable harvest and secure a future where agriculture thrives in harmony with our planet.

4.2 Advancements in Aquaculture: Sustainable Practices for the Blue Economy

Aquaculture, or the farming of aquatic organisms such as fish, crustaceans, molluscs, and aquatic plants, has emerged as a vital component of global food security. As the demand for seafood increases and wild fish stocks dwindle, sustainable aquaculture practices are essential for meeting this demand while minimizing environmental impacts. This section looks at some of the latest advancements in aquaculture, highlighting sustainable practices that are revolutionizing the blue economy.

The Importance of Sustainable Aquaculture
Sustainable aquaculture is critical for several reasons. Firstly, it helps alleviate pressure on overfished wild populations, allowing ecosystems to recover and maintain biodiversity. Secondly, it provides a reliable source of protein for a growing global population. Lastly, sustainable aquaculture practices can contribute to local economies, providing jobs and supporting livelihoods in coastal and rural communities.

Innovations in Feed and Nutrition
One of the significant challenges in aquaculture is the reliance on fishmeal and fish oil, which are derived from wild-caught fish, thus contributing to overfishing. Innovations in feed and nutrition have led to the development of alternative protein sources, such as plant-based feeds, insect meal, and microbial proteins. These alternatives not only reduce the dependency on wild fish stocks but also have a lower environmental footprint.

Plant-Based Feeds
Plant-based feeds, derived from crops like soy, corn, and wheat, are increasingly being used as substitutes for fishmeal. Advances in genetic engineering and biotechnology have improved the nutritional profiles of these plants, making them suitable for aquaculture. However, it is essential to ensure that the cultivation of these crops does not lead to deforestation or other unsustainable practices.

Insect Meal
Insects, such as black soldier fly larvae, are rich in protein and can be farmed sustainably. They can be fed on organic waste, converting it into high-quality protein for aquaculture feeds. This not only addresses the issue of waste management but also provides a circular economy solution.

Microbial Proteins
Microbial proteins, produced from bacteria, yeast, and algae, are another promising alternative. These proteins can be grown using renewable energy sources and agricultural by-products, reducing their environmental impact. Research is ongoing to optimize the nutritional content and cost-effectiveness of microbial proteins for widespread use in aquaculture.

Advances in Breeding and Genetics
Selective breeding and genetic improvement are powerful tools for enhancing the productivity and sustainability of aquaculture. Advances in these areas have led to the development of disease-resistant, fast-growing, and feed-

efficient aquatic species.

Selective Breeding
Selective breeding involves choosing the best-performing individuals to reproduce, thereby passing on desirable traits to the next generation. This traditional method has been used for centuries in agriculture and is now being applied to aquaculture. By selecting traits such as growth rate, feed conversion efficiency, and disease resistance, aquaculture producers can improve the overall productivity and sustainability of their operations.

Genetic Engineering and CRISPR
Genetic engineering and CRISPR (Clustered Regularly Interspaced Short Palindromic Repeats) technology offer more precise and targeted methods for enhancing aquaculture species. These techniques allow scientists to introduce specific genes that confer desirable traits, such as increased growth rates or resistance to diseases and environmental stressors. CRISPR technology has the potential to improve aquaculture production; however, public and regulatory acceptance is the key to its potential being realized (Okoli et al., 2021). CRISPR applications remain mostly at the research stage, and in aquaculture breeding programs, it is still limited. While the use of genetic engineering in aquaculture is still a topic of debate, it holds significant potential for improving sustainability.

Integrated Multi-Trophic Aquaculture (IMTA)
Integrated Multi-Trophic Aquaculture (IMTA) is an innovative approach that involves cultivating different species together in a way that mimics natural ecosystems. In IMTA systems, the waste produced by one species serves as a nutrient source for another, creating a balanced and sustainable system.

How IMTA Works
Mainly in the United States and Canada, IMTA is an evolving approach to seafood production that utilizes an ecosystem-management approach where 'fed' species, such as finfish or shrimp, are farmed near species that can 'extract' nutrients from the water column, such as shellfish and algae or seaweed.

In a typical IMTA system, fish or shrimp are farmed alongside seaweed and filter-feeding bivalves like mussels or oysters. The waste produced by the fish provides nutrients for the seaweed, which in turn helps to absorb excess nutrients and improve water quality. The bivalves filter the water, removing particulate matter and further enhancing water clarity.

Benefits of IMTA
IMTA offers several environmental and economic benefits. It reduces the environmental impact of aquaculture by recycling nutrients and minimizing waste. It also diversifies production, providing multiple revenue streams for farmers. Additionally, IMTA systems can enhance ecosystem services, such as water purification and habitat provision, contributing to the overall health of coastal environments.

Recirculating Aquaculture Systems (RAS)
Recirculating Aquaculture Systems (RAS) are land-based systems that recycle water within the facility, reducing the need for large volumes of fresh water and minimizing the risk of disease outbreaks. RAS technology has seen significant advancements in recent years, making it a viable option for sustainable aquaculture.

How RAS Works
In a RAS, water from the fish tanks is filtered and treated to remove waste products before being recirculated back into the tanks. This closed-loop system allows for precise control over water quality parameters, such as temperature, pH, and dissolved oxygen levels, creating optimal conditions for fish growth.

Advantages of RAS
RAS offers several advantages over traditional open-water systems. It significantly reduces water usage and the risk of disease transmission, as the water is continuously treated and recycled. RAS also minimizes the environmental impact of aquaculture by preventing the release of waste and chemicals into natural water bodies. Additionally, RAS can be located closer to markets, reducing transportation costs and carbon emissions.

Aquaponics: Combining Aquaculture and Hydroponics
Aquaponics is a sustainable farming method that combines aquaculture with hydroponics—the cultivation of plants in water. In an aquaponic system, the waste produced by the fish provides nutrients for the plants, while the plants help to filter and clean the water for the fish.

How Aquaponics Works
In an aquaponic system, fish are raised in tanks, and their waste is converted by beneficial bacteria into nutrients that are taken up by the plants. The plants

are grown in soilless systems, such as nutrient film technique (NFT) or deep water culture (DWC), and help to purify the water before it is returned to the fish tanks. This creates a closed-loop system that efficiently uses resources and minimizes waste.

Benefits of Aquaponics
Aquaponics offers several sustainability benefits. It uses significantly less water than traditional soil-based agriculture, as the water is continuously recycled within the system. It also eliminates the need for chemical fertilizers, as the fish waste provides all the necessary nutrients for plant growth. Additionally, aquaponics can be implemented in urban areas, reducing the need for transportation and providing fresh, locally-grown produce.

Sustainable Practices in Marine Aquaculture

Marine aquaculture, or mariculture, involves the farming of marine species in ocean environments. Sustainable practices in mariculture are essential for protecting marine ecosystems and ensuring the long-term viability of the industry.

Off-Shore Aquaculture
Off-shore aquaculture involves farming species in deeper, open-ocean environments, away from sensitive coastal areas. This method reduces the impact on coastal ecosystems and allows for the cultivation of larger volumes of seafood. Advances in cage design and mooring systems have made off-shore aquaculture more feasible and sustainable.

Shellfish Farming
Shellfish farming, including the cultivation of oysters, mussels, and clams, is inherently sustainable. Shellfish are filter feeders that improve water quality by removing excess nutrients and particulate matter. They also provide important habitat for other marine species. Sustainable shellfish farming practices include selecting appropriate sites, minimizing habitat disruption, and using biodegradable materials for farming equipment.

The Future of Sustainable Aquaculture – Balance & Sustainability

The advancements in sustainable aquaculture practices and technologies are paving the way for a more resilient and environmentally friendly blue economy.

By reducing dependency on wild fish stocks, improving feed and nutrition, enhancing breeding and genetics, and implementing innovative farming systems like IMTA, RAS, and aquaponics, the aquaculture industry can meet the growing demand for seafood while protecting our planet's precious aquatic ecosystems.

Policymakers, investors, and entrepreneurs must continue to support, develop and promote these sustainable practices to ensure a thriving future for aquaculture and the communities that depend on it.

4.3 Renewable Energy for Agriculture & Aquaculture

The integration of renewable energy solutions within the agriculture and aquaculture sectors represents a pivotal shift towards more sustainable and resilient practices. As the world grapples with the dual challenges of climate change and food security, the adoption of renewable energy technologies offers a viable pathway to reduce carbon footprints, enhance energy efficiency, and secure long-term economic and environmental benefits. This section delves into the various renewable energy solutions that are revolutionizing these sectors, highlighting their applications, benefits, and the challenges that must be navigated to achieve widespread adoption.

Solar Power: Harnessing the Sun's Energy

Solar Photovoltaic (PV) Systems

Solar photovoltaic (PV) systems are becoming increasingly prevalent in agricultural and aquaculture operations. These systems convert sunlight directly into electricity, providing a clean and renewable energy source that can power a wide range of equipment and processes.

In agriculture, solar PV systems can be used to power irrigation pumps, greenhouse lighting, and temperature control systems. In aquaculture, they can support aeration systems, water pumps, and other essential functions.

One of the significant advantages of solar PV systems is their scalability. They can be deployed in small-scale farms and large agricultural enterprises alike, tailored to meet specific energy needs. Additionally, advancements in solar technology, such as bifacial panels and solar tracking systems, have significantly increased the efficiency and energy output of PV installations.

Solar Water Heating Systems

Solar water heating systems are another valuable application of solar energy in agriculture and aquaculture. These systems use solar collectors to capture and convert sunlight into heat, which is then used to warm water for various purposes. In agriculture, solar-heated water can be used for livestock drinking water, cleaning, and sanitizing equipment. In aquaculture, it can maintain optimal water temperatures in fish ponds and tanks, promoting healthier and faster-growing aquatic species.

The benefits of solar water heating systems extend beyond energy savings. They also contribute to reducing greenhouse gas emissions and reliance on fossil fuels, aligning with broader ESG goals. Furthermore, these systems often have a relatively short payback period, making them an economically attractive option for many operations.

Wind Power: Capturing the Power of the Wind
Wind Turbines

Wind power, harnessed through the use of wind turbines, offers another promising renewable energy solution for agriculture and aquaculture. Wind turbines convert the kinetic energy of wind into mechanical power, which can then be used to generate electricity. In agricultural settings, wind turbines can power irrigation systems, grain mills, and other electrically driven equipment. In coastal or offshore aquaculture operations, wind energy can support lighting, water circulation, and other critical functions.

The deployment of wind turbines in agricultural and aquaculture operations can significantly reduce energy costs and enhance energy security. Moreover, wind power generation produces no greenhouse gas emissions, contributing to the reduction of the carbon footprint of these sectors. However, the feasibility of wind energy projects depends on several factors, including wind availability, turbine placement, and regulatory considerations.

Hybrid Systems: Integrating Wind and Solar
Hybrid renewable energy systems, which combine wind and solar power, offer a synergistic approach to maximizing energy generation and reliability. By integrating wind turbines and solar PV, or PVT panels to heat water, these systems can provide a more consistent and reliable energy supply, as the two energy sources often complement each other. For instance, solar panels can generate electricity during sunny days, while wind turbines can produce power during windy conditions, including at night.

Hybrid systems can be particularly beneficial in remote or off-grid agricultural and aquaculture operations, where access to a stable and reliable energy supply is crucial. These systems can reduce the reliance on diesel generators and other non-renewable energy sources, further promoting sustainability and cost savings.

Biomass Energy: Turning Waste into Power

Biomass Feedstocks

Biomass energy utilizes organic materials, such as crop residues, animal manure, and other agricultural by-products, to produce heat, electricity, or biofuels. This renewable energy source offers a unique advantage in agriculture and aquaculture by turning waste products into valuable energy resources. Common biomass feedstocks include corn stover, rice husks, and livestock manure, among others.

The use of biomass energy can significantly reduce waste disposal costs and environmental impacts, while also providing a renewable and locally-sourced energy supply. In addition, the production of biofuels from biomass can create new revenue streams for farmers and aquaculture operators, further enhancing the economic sustainability of their operations.

Anaerobic Digestion

Anaerobic digestion is a widely used technology for converting biomass feedstocks into biogas, a renewable energy source composed primarily of methane and carbon dioxide. This technology utilises the natural microbial breakdown of organic materials in the absence of oxygen, to produce biogas and digestate, a nutrient-rich clay-type by-product that can be used as fertilizer.

Anaerobic digestion systems can be implemented on farms and aquaculture facilities to process animal manure, crop residues, and other organic wastes. The biogas produced can be used for heating, electricity generation, or as a vehicle fuel, while the digestate can be applied to fields to enhance soil fertility and crop yields. This closed-loop approach contributes to the circular economy and reduces the environmental footprint of agricultural and aquaculture operations.

Geothermal Energy: Tapping into the Earth's Heat

Ground-Source Heat Pumps

Geothermal energy, derived from the heat stored within the Earth's crust, offers another innovative solution for sustainable agriculture and aquaculture. Ground-source heat pumps (GSHPs) harness this geothermal energy to provide heating and cooling for buildings, greenhouses, and aquaculture facilities. These systems work by transferring heat between the ground and the building through a network of buried pipes, known as a ground loop.

GSHPs are highly efficient and can provide significant energy savings compared to conventional heating and cooling systems. In agriculture, they can maintain optimal temperatures in greenhouses, improving plant growth and productivity. In aquaculture, they can regulate water temperatures in fish tanks and ponds, supporting the health and growth of aquatic species.

Direct-Use Applications
Direct-use applications of geothermal energy involve the direct extraction and use of geothermal fluids for heating purposes. In agriculture, direct-use geothermal energy can be utilized for soil warming, greenhouse heating, and drying crops. In aquaculture, it can be used to maintain consistent water temperatures in fish ponds and hatcheries, enhancing the growth and health of aquatic species.

The advantages of direct-use geothermal energy include its low operating costs and minimal environmental impact. However, the feasibility of geothermal projects depends on the availability of suitable geothermal resources and the initial investment required for drilling and infrastructure development.

Innovations in Renewable Energy Storage

Battery Storage Systems
One of the key challenges in integrating renewable energy solutions into agriculture and aquaculture is the intermittent nature of energy sources like solar and wind. Battery storage systems offer a solution to this challenge by storing excess energy generated during peak production periods and releasing it when energy demand is high or generation is low. Lithium-ion batteries are currently the most common storage technology, but advancements in alternative battery chemistries, such as flow batteries and solid-state batteries, are expanding the options available.

Battery storage systems enhance the reliability and resilience of renewable energy systems, ensuring a stable and continuous energy supply. They can also provide backup power during grid outages, reducing the vulnerability of agricultural and aquaculture operations to energy disruptions. Furthermore, battery storage can facilitate the integration of hybrid renewable energy systems, optimizing energy generation and usage.

Thermal Energy Storage
Thermal energy storage (TES) is another innovative solution for managing the

variability of renewable energy sources. TES systems store excess thermal energy in various forms, such as hot water, molten salts, or phase-change materials, and release it when needed. In agriculture, TES can be used to store solar thermal energy for greenhouse heating or crop drying. In aquaculture, it can maintain consistent water temperatures in fish tanks and ponds, even during periods of low solar or wind energy generation.

The adoption of TES systems can improve the efficiency and sustainability of renewable energy applications in agriculture and aquaculture. By providing a reliable and flexible energy storage solution, TES can help stabilize energy supply and demand, reduce energy costs, and enhance the overall resilience of these sectors.

Policy and Financial Incentives
The successful adoption of renewable energy solutions in agriculture and aquaculture often depends on supportive policy frameworks and financial incentives. Governments around the world are implementing various programs and subsidies to encourage the use of renewable energy in these sectors. These incentives can include tax credits, grants, low-interest loans, and feed-in tariffs that guarantee a fixed price for renewable energy generated and fed into the grid.

By providing financial support and reducing the initial investment barriers, these incentives can accelerate the adoption of renewable energy technologies and promote sustainable practices. Policymakers play a crucial role in designing and implementing these programs, ensuring they are accessible and effectively address the needs of agricultural and aquaculture operators.

Private Sector Investment
In addition to government incentives, private sector investment is essential for scaling renewable energy solutions in agriculture and aquaculture. Investors are increasingly recognizing the economic and environmental benefits of renewable energy projects, driving capital towards these initiatives. Public-private partnerships, venture capital, and impact investing are some of the mechanisms through which private-sector funds can be mobilized to support renewable energy development.

Collaboration between the public and private sectors can create a conducive environment for innovation and growth, fostering the widespread adoption of renewable energy technologies. By aligning financial interests with sustainability goals, these partnerships can drive impactful change and contribute to the long-term resilience of the agriculture and aquaculture sectors.

Conclusion: A Sustainable Future
The integration of renewable energy solutions in agriculture and aquaculture holds immense potential to transform these sectors, making them more sustainable, resilient, and economically viable. By harnessing the power of the sun, wind, biomass, and geothermal energy, agricultural and aquaculture operations can reduce their environmental footprint, enhance energy efficiency, and secure long-term benefits.

However, achieving this vision requires concerted efforts from policymakers, investors, entrepreneurs, and practitioners. Through innovation, collaboration, and strategic investment, we can pave the way for a sustainable harvest that thrives in harmony with our planet.

4.4 Blockchain - Transparency & Traceability in the Food Supply Chain
Blockchain technology, originally developed as the backbone for cryptocurrencies like Bitcoin, has found a promising application in the agricultural sector.

While all but invisible to mere mortals, the decentralized, immutable ledger system offered by blockchain will revolutionize the way we manage and monitor the food supply chain. This section delves into how blockchain ensures transparency and traceability, ultimately fostering trust and sustainability in agriculture.

Understanding Blockchain Technology
At its core, blockchain is a distributed ledger technology that records transactions across multiple computers so that the record cannot be altered retroactively. Each 'block' contains a list of transactions, and these blocks are linked chronologically to form a 'chain.' This decentralized nature ensures that no single entity has control over the entire blockchain, making it highly secure and resistant to tampering.

The Need for Transparency and Traceability
In today's globalized world, the food supply chain is incredibly complex, involving numerous stakeholders from farmers to processors, distributors,

retailers, and consumers. This complexity often leads to issues like food fraud such as, for example, well-known honey and maple syrup adulteration cases, contamination, and inefficiencies. Traditional systems to manage the supply chain rely heavily on paper-based records, which are prone to errors and manipulation. Blockchain technology addresses these challenges by providing an immutable, transparent, and traceable record of every transaction in the supply chain.

How Blockchain Enhances Transparency
Immutable Records
One of the key features of blockchain is its immutability. Once a transaction is recorded, it cannot be altered or deleted. This ensures that all stakeholders have access to accurate and unalterable information, thereby enhancing transparency. For instance, a farmer can record the harvest date, type of crop, and use of pesticides, which can then be verified by other stakeholders in the chain.

Decentralized Validation
Blockchain operates on a decentralized network where each participant has a copy of the ledger. Transactions are validated through consensus mechanisms, ensuring that no single party can manipulate the data. This decentralized validation process builds trust among stakeholders, as everyone has access to the same information.

Real-time Monitoring
Blockchain allows for real-time monitoring of the supply chain. Sensors and IoT devices can be integrated with blockchain to automatically record data such as temperature, humidity, and location during transportation and storage. This real-time data can be accessed by all stakeholders, ensuring that any issues can be promptly addressed.

Traceability: From Farm to Fork
Provenance Tracking
Blockchain enables detailed provenance tracking, allowing consumers to trace the journey of their food from the farm to their plate. Each transaction, from planting and harvesting to processing and distribution, is recorded on the blockchain. Consumers can scan a QR code on the product packaging to access this information, providing them with assurance about the origin and quality of their food.

Combatting Food Fraud
Food fraud, such as mislabelling and adulteration, is a significant concern in the food industry. Blockchain's immutable records make it difficult for bad actors to alter information about the product's origin, ingredients, or processing methods. This enhances the integrity of the supply chain and helps combat food fraud.

Enhancing Food Safety
Traceability is crucial for ensuring food safety. In the event of a contamination outbreak, blockchain allows for quick identification of the affected batches and their origins. This rapid traceability can significantly reduce the time required for recalls, minimizing the impact on public health and reducing financial losses for companies.

Case Studies: Blockchain in Action

IBM Food Trust
IBM Food Trust is one of the most prominent examples of blockchain implementation in the food supply chain. The platform has been adopted by major players like Walmart, Nestlé, and Dole. By using blockchain, these companies have improved their supply chain transparency, reduced food waste, and enhanced food safety. For instance, Walmart requires its leafy green suppliers to use IBM Food Trust, enabling rapid traceability from farm to store.

The declared objective of IBM Food Trust is to "Share food information securely and boost transparency in the global food chain with a modular, blockchain-based food safety and traceability solution."

Provenance
Provenance is a UK-based company that leverages blockchain to provide transparency in supply chains across various industries, including agriculture. Their platform allows consumers to verify the ethical and sustainable practices of the brands they purchase from.

For example, Provenance partnered with a coffee company to trace the beans from farm to cup, ensuring fair trade practices and sustainability. Food provenance essentially means knowing where food was grown, caught or raised, knowing how that food was produced and how the resulting food products were transported.

Challenges and Solutions
Scalability
One of the primary challenges of blockchain technology is scalability. As the number of transactions increases, the blockchain can become slow and inefficient. To address this, solutions like sharding and off-chain transactions are being explored. Sharding involves breaking the blockchain into smaller, more manageable pieces, while off-chain transactions allow for some transactions to be processed outside the main blockchain, reducing the load.

Interoperability
The lack of standardization and interoperability between different blockchain platforms can hinder widespread adoption. Developing common standards and protocols is crucial for ensuring that different systems can communicate and work together seamlessly.

Organizations like the Blockchain in Transport Alliance (BiTA), founded in 2017, are working towards creating such standards. BiTA members, with over 500 members in over 25 countries, are leading the effort "to develop and embrace a common framework and standards" from which transportation, logistics, supply chain, and freight marketplace participants can build revolutionary blockchain and distributed ledger technology (DLT) applications.

Initial Costs
Implementing blockchain technology can require significant upfront investment in terms of infrastructure and training. However, the long-term benefits, such as reduced fraud, improved efficiency, and enhanced consumer trust, can outweigh these initial costs. Governments and industry bodies can also play a role in supporting and subsidizing the adoption of blockchain in agriculture.

Future Prospects
Integration with IoT and AI
The integration of blockchain with Internet of Things (IoT) devices and Artificial Intelligence (AI) can further enhance the capabilities of the food supply chain. IoT devices can automatically record data on the blockchain, while AI can analyse this data to optimize supply chain operations, predict demand, and identify potential issues before they become major problems.

Smart Contracts
Smart contracts are self-executing contracts with the terms of the agreement

directly written into code. They can automate various processes in the supply chain, such as payments, quality checks, and compliance with regulations. For example, a smart contract could automatically release payment to a farmer once the delivery of crops is confirmed and verified on the blockchain.

Consumer Engagement
As consumers become more conscious of the ethical and environmental impact of their purchases, blockchain can provide them with the transparency they seek. Brands can use blockchain to showcase their sustainable practices, engage with consumers, and build brand loyalty. This increased consumer trust can translate into higher sales and a competitive advantage in the market.

Blockchain technology holds immense potential to transform the food supply chain by enhancing transparency and traceability. While there are challenges to overcome, the benefits far outweigh the drawbacks. As the technology matures and more stakeholders adopt blockchain, we can expect a more efficient, trustworthy, and sustainable food supply chain. Policymakers, investors, and entrepreneurs must recognize the value of blockchain and work towards its widespread implementation to secure a greener, more resilient future for agriculture.

4.5 Harnessing Innovation for a Sustainable Future

As we navigate the intersection of agriculture and Environmental, Social, and Governance (ESG) principles, it is clear that innovation is our most powerful ally. Cutting-edge technologies such as precision farming, IoT, and AI are revolutionizing how we approach agricultural productivity and sustainability. These advancements enable more efficient resource use, reducing waste and environmental impact while boosting yields.

In the realm of aquaculture, sustainable practices are leading the charge towards a more resilient blue economy. By adopting advanced techniques and technologies, we can ensure the health of aquatic ecosystems and the communities that depend on them.

Renewable energy solutions are equally pivotal, providing sustainable power sources for both agriculture and aquaculture. Embracing solar, wind, and bioenergy not only reduces carbon footprints but also enhances energy security and operational efficiency.

The integration of blockchain technology offers unparalleled transparency and traceability in the food supply chain. This fosters trust among consumers and stakeholders, ensuring that ethical and sustainable practices are upheld from farm to fork.

Key Takeaways and Actionable Advice:
1. Embrace precision farming and AI to optimize resource use and increase agricultural productivity.
2. Adopt sustainable aquaculture practices to support the blue economy and protect aquatic ecosystems.
3. Invest in renewable energy solutions to power agricultural and aquacultural operations sustainably.
4. Implement blockchain technology to enhance transparency and traceability in the food supply chain.

By leveraging these innovations and technologies, we can create a more sustainable and equitable future for agriculture and aquaculture, aligning our practices with ESG principles and ensuring long-term resilience and prosperity.

5 STRATEGIC ROADMAP FOR POLICY MAKERS AND ENTREPRENEURS

Source: Pexels - Photo by Johannes Plenio

In the intricate tapestry of sustainable agriculture, policy makers and entrepreneurs occupy pivotal roles. Their decisions and innovations form the backbone of a resilient and sustainable food supply chain, one that can withstand the multifaceted challenges of our era.

As we stand on the precipice of a new agricultural revolution, this chapter delves into the strategic roadmap necessary to usher in an era where agriculture and ESG principles are inextricably linked, ensuring a greener and more prosperous future. The urgency to develop and implement policies that bolster sustainable agricultural practices has never been more pronounced. Climate change, resource depletion, and socio-economic disparities necessitate a rethinking of traditional agricultural paradigms.

Policymakers are tasked with the formidable challenge of creating frameworks that not only support but actively encourage sustainable practices. This involves a delicate balance of regulation, incentives, and awareness campaigns aimed at transforming both the mindset and methodology of agricultural stakeholders. In this chapter, we will explore the crucial aspects of policy development, focusing on how to craft legislation that fosters innovation, supports farmers, and ensures environmental stewardship.

Public-private partnerships emerge as a cornerstone in this endeavor. The synergy between governmental bodies and private enterprises can catalyze sustainable growth, driving forward initiatives that neither party could achieve independently. These collaborations can unlock new funding streams, introduce cutting-edge technologies, and scale sustainable practices more effectively. We will examine some successful case studies, extract key lessons that can be applied to future partnerships, and highlight the mutual benefits and shared responsibilities of such alliances.

For entrepreneurs, the sustainable agriculture market presents a fertile ground for innovation and profit. However, navigating this sector requires a keen understanding of developments in both market dynamics and ESG principles. This chapter provides a few entrepreneurial strategies tailored to entering and thriving in the sustainable agriculture market. From identifying lucrative niches, to leveraging green technologies, we offer a quick guide for those building successful, sustainable enterprises. Entrepreneurs will find actionable insights on how to align their business models with ESG criteria, attract impact investors, and cultivate a brand that resonates with the growing eco-conscious consumer base.

Looking ahead, the integration of ESG principles in agriculture is not just a trend but a necessity for survival. Future outlooks predict a landscape where sustainability is the norm, driven by regulatory pressures, consumer demand, and technological advancements. We will explore the emerging trends and predictions for sustainable agriculture, offering a glimpse into what the future holds. From advancements in precision farming to the increasing relevance of blockchain in supply chain transparency, this chapter paints a picture of a future where innovation and sustainability go hand in hand.

In conclusion, Chapter 5 provides a strategic roadmap for policymakers and entrepreneurs at the forefront of the sustainable agriculture movement. It is a call to action, urging these key players to harness their influence and creativity to drive impactful change. By developing forward-thinking policies, forging robust public-private partnerships, and adopting innovative business strategies, we can collectively work towards "a more sustainable harvest".

Together, we can secure a future where agriculture not only feeds the world but does so in harmony with our planet.

5.1 Crafting Policies for a Greener Tomorrow: Supporting Sustainable Agricultural Practices

Sustainable agriculture is more than a trend; it is an imperative for ensuring global food security and environmental health in the 21st century. As such, the role of policymakers and entrepreneurs cannot be overstated in driving this transformative agenda. Policies that support sustainable agricultural practices are crucial to creating an ecosystem where innovation flourishes, resources are utilized efficiently, and the socio-economic fabric of rural communities is strengthened.

Understanding the Importance of Sustainable Agricultural Policies

Sustainable agricultural policies provide a framework for balancing the economic, environmental, and social dimensions of agricultural production. They are designed to promote practices that enhance productivity while minimizing the environmental footprint, ensuring that farming remains viable for future generations.

These policies encompass a range of strategies, including incentives for sustainable practices, regulations to protect natural resources, and support for research and development in sustainable technologies.

Policy Framework:
Key Elements Effective policies for sustainable agriculture typically include several key elements:

1. Economic Incentives: Financial incentives such as subsidies, grants, and tax breaks can encourage farmers to adopt sustainable practices. These economic tools are vital for offsetting the initial costs of transitioning to more sustainable methods.
2. Regulatory Measures: Regulations play a crucial role in ensuring compliance with environmental standards. This includes setting limits on the use of chemical inputs, mandating conservation practices, and enforcing penalties for non-compliance.
3. Support for Research and Innovation: Investment in research and development is essential for advancing sustainable agricultural technologies. Policies should support public and private sector research initiatives and promote the dissemination of knowledge and best practices.
4. Infrastructure Development: Building robust infrastructure, such as

irrigation systems, storage facilities, and transportation networks, is crucial for supporting sustainable agriculture. Policies should prioritize infrastructure projects that enhance efficiency and reduce environmental impacts.
5. Education and Training: Providing farmers with the knowledge and skills needed to implement sustainable practices is vital. Policies should support educational programs, extension services, and training initiatives that empower farmers to make informed decisions.

Economic Incentives - Catalyzing Change

Economic incentives are one of the most effective tools for encouraging the adoption of sustainable agricultural practices. They can take various forms, including direct payments, subsidies, low-interest loans, and tax incentives. By reducing the financial burden of transitioning to sustainable methods, these incentives make it more feasible for farmers to invest in practices that benefit the environment and society.

Subsidies and Grants
Subsidies and grants are direct financial support provided to farmers to help them adopt sustainable practices. These can be used to cover the costs of purchasing eco-friendly equipment, implementing soil conservation measures, or transitioning to organic farming. For example, a government might offer grants to farmers who install solar-powered irrigation systems or adopt crop rotation practices that enhance soil health.

Tax Incentives
Tax incentives, such as deductions, credits, and exemptions, can also encourage sustainable practices. For instance, farmers who invest in renewable energy sources or implement water-saving technologies could be eligible for tax breaks. These incentives not only reduce the financial burden on farmers but also signal the government's commitment to promoting sustainability.

Low-Interest Loans
Access to affordable financing is critical for farmers looking to adopt sustainable practices. Low-interest loans can provide the necessary capital for investments in sustainable technologies, such as precision agriculture tools or organic fertilizers. By offering favorable loan terms, policymakers can make it easier for farmers to secure the funding they need to transition to more sustainable methods.

Regulatory Measures: Setting Standards

While economic incentives can encourage the voluntary adoption of sustainable practices, regulatory measures are necessary to ensure compliance and protect natural resources. Regulations set clear standards for environmental performance and hold farmers accountable for their practices.

Environmental Compliance Standards

Environmental compliance standards are regulations that set limits on the use of chemical inputs, such as pesticides and fertilizers, to prevent pollution and protect ecosystems. These standards can also mandate conservation practices, such as maintaining buffer zones around water bodies or implementing erosion control measures. By enforcing these standards, policymakers can ensure that agricultural activities do not harm the environment.

Penalties for Non-Compliance

To ensure that regulations are effective, it is important to have a system of penalties for non-compliance. These penalties can include fines, loss of subsidies, or even suspension of farming licenses. By holding farmers accountable for their environmental impact, policymakers can create a culture of responsibility and stewardship.

Support for Research and Innovation - Driving Progress

Research and innovation are the backbone of sustainable agriculture. Policies that support research and development can accelerate the discovery of new technologies and practices that enhance sustainability.

Public and Private Sector Collaboration

Collaboration between the public and private sectors is essential for advancing sustainable agricultural research. Governments can fund research initiatives at universities and research institutions, while also encouraging private sector investment in agricultural innovation. Public-private partnerships can facilitate the development and commercialization of new technologies that address sustainability challenges.

Knowledge Dissemination and Extension Services

Once new technologies and practices are developed, it is important to ensure that farmers have access to this knowledge. Extension services, which provide education and technical assistance to farmers, play a crucial role in disseminating information about sustainable practices.

Policies should support the expansion of extension services and the development of online platforms that provide farmers with access to the latest research and best practices.

Infrastructure Development - Building a Sustainable Foundation
Infrastructure is a critical component of sustainable agriculture. Policies that prioritize the development of infrastructure can enhance efficiency, reduce environmental impacts, and improve the resilience of agricultural systems.

Water Storage, Harvesting & Irrigation Systems
Efficient irrigation systems are essential for sustainable water management. Policies should support the development and maintenance of irrigation infrastructure that minimizes water waste and enhances water use efficiency. This can include the promotion of drip irrigation systems, which deliver water directly to plant roots, reducing evaporation and runoff.

Storage and Transportation
Proper storage and transportation infrastructure is vital for reducing food waste and ensuring that agricultural products reach markets in good condition. Policies should prioritize the development of storage facilities, such as cold storage units, that preserve the quality of perishable goods.

Additionally, investments in transportation networks can improve market access for farmers and reduce the carbon footprint of agricultural supply chains.

Renewable Energy Infrastructure
Renewable energy sources, such as solar and wind power, can reduce the environmental impact of agricultural activities. Policies should support the development of renewable energy infrastructure on farms, including the installation of solar panels and wind turbines.

By providing incentives for renewable energy adoption, policymakers can help farmers reduce their reliance on fossil fuels and lower their greenhouse gas emissions.

Education and Training - Empowering Farmers
Education and training are essential for empowering farmers to adopt sustainable practices. Policies that support educational initiatives can provide farmers with the knowledge and skills they need to make informed decisions and implement effective sustainability measures.

Green from Green II - Businesses & Utilities

Education Programs
Farmer education programs can cover a wide range of topics, including soil health, water management, integrated pest management, and organic farming. These programs can be delivered through workshops, field days, and online courses. By providing farmers with access to education, policymakers can help them stay informed about the latest research and best practices in sustainable agriculture.

Extension Services
Extension services play a crucial role in providing technical assistance and support to farmers. These services can offer one-on-one consultations, field demonstrations, and training sessions to help farmers implement sustainable practices. Policies should support the expansion of extension services to ensure that all farmers have access to the resources they need.

Training for Young Farmers
Engaging the next generation of farmers is vital for the future of sustainable agriculture. Policies should support training programs for young farmers, including apprenticeships, mentorship opportunities, and agricultural education in schools. By investing in the education of young farmers, policymakers can ensure that the principles of sustainability are passed on to future generations.

A Collective Effort for a Sustainable Future

The development of policies that support sustainable agricultural practices is a collective effort that requires the collaboration of governments, farmers, researchers, and the private sector.

By implementing economic incentives, regulatory measures, support for research and innovation, infrastructure development, and education and training programs, policymakers can create an environment where sustainable agriculture thrives.

As we look to the future, sustainable agriculture is not just an option, but an imperative given the extent and effects of climate change in recent years. The policies and initiatives that we develop today will shape the agricultural landscape of tomorrow, ensuring that we can meet the needs of a growing population while preserving the health of our planet.

By working together, we can build a more sustainable, resilient, and prosperous agricultural system for future generations.

5.2 Public-Private Partnerships: Collaborate for Sustainable Growth

In the evolving landscape of sustainable agriculture, public-private partnerships (PPPs) have emerged as a pivotal mechanism for driving growth in the sector. These collaborations leverage the strengths of both sectors—governmental resources, regulatory frameworks, and public interest focus combined with private sector innovation, efficiency, and capital. This symbiotic relationship can be instrumental in fostering a resilient agricultural ecosystem to not only meet the demands of today but also safeguard tomorrow.

Public-private partnerships in sustainable agriculture are multifaceted, addressing various aspects from research and development to infrastructure, market access, and policy formulation. By uniting diverse stakeholders, PPPs create a platform for shared risk, pooled resources, and collective expertise, leading to more robust and scalable solutions.

Harnessing Innovation and Technology

One of the most significant advantages of PPPs is the ability to harness innovation and technology. The private sector, driven by competition and profit motives, often spearheads technological advancements. These innovations—ranging from precision farming and biotechnology to advanced data analytics and automation—are critical in enhancing agricultural productivity and sustainability. However, the adoption of such technologies can be slow without the support and facilitation of the public sector.

Through PPPs, governments can provide the necessary infrastructure, regulatory support, and funding to accelerate the deployment of cutting-edge technologies in agriculture. For instance, joint ventures can be established to develop and disseminate sustainable farming practices, such as precision agriculture, which optimizes resource use and minimizes environmental impact.

Public entities can also facilitate training and capacity-building programs to ensure that farmers and agricultural workers are well-equipped to utilize new technologies effectively.

<u>Case Study: The Agri-Tech Partnership</u>
A notable example of a successful PPP in this domain is the Agri-Tech Partnership, a collaboration between governmental agricultural departments

and leading Agri-tech firms. This initiative focuses on integrating advanced technologies like IoT (Internet of Things) sensors, drone monitoring, and AI-driven analytics into mainstream farming practices. The partnership has resulted in significant improvements in crop yields, resource efficiency, and environmental sustainability.

The government's role in this partnership includes providing grants and subsidies for technology adoption, setting up pilot projects to demonstrate the benefits of these technologies, and creating an enabling regulatory environment. On the other hand, private partners contribute technological expertise, innovation, and investment. The collaboration also extends to research institutions, which play a crucial role in developing and validating new technologies.

Building Sustainable Supply Chains

PPPs are also instrumental in building sustainable supply chains. The complexity and interdependence of modern agricultural supply chains necessitate a collaborative approach to ensure sustainability at every stage—from production and processing to distribution and consumption.

Sustainable Logistics and Transportation

One critical area where PPPs can make a significant impact is in logistics and transportation. The private sector, with its operational efficiency and logistical expertise, can work alongside public entities to develop sustainable transportation networks that reduce carbon footprints and enhance the efficiency of agricultural supply chains. For example, partnerships can be formed to invest in green transportation solutions, such as electric and hybrid vehicles, as well as infrastructure for cold chain logistics to minimize food wastage.

Governments can incentivize these investments through tax breaks, subsidies, and favorable policies, while private companies bring in the necessary capital and operational capabilities.

Financing Sustainable Agriculture

Access to finance is a critical challenge for sustainable agriculture, particularly for small and medium-sized enterprises (SMEs) and smallholder farmers.

PPPs can play a crucial role in bridging this financing gap by pooling public and private sector resources to create innovative financial instruments and mechanisms.

Blended Finance Models
Blended finance models, which combine public funding with private investment, are an effective tool for financing sustainable agriculture. These models leverage public funds to de-risk private investments, making it more attractive for private investors to finance sustainable agricultural projects.

For example, a government could establish a risk-sharing facility that provides guarantees or first-loss capital to private investors in sustainable agriculture projects. This reduces the perceived risk for private investors, encouraging them to invest in projects they might otherwise consider too risky.

Additionally, public funds can be used to provide concessional loans or grants to support the initial stages of sustainable agricultural ventures.

Enhancing Market Access and Fair Trade

Market access is another critical area where PPPs can make a substantial difference. Sustainable agriculture often involves smallholder farmers and SMEs that struggle to access markets due to various barriers, including lack of infrastructure, market information, and bargaining power.

Building Market Linkages
PPPs can facilitate the development of market linkages that connect smallholder farmers and SMEs with larger markets, both domestically and internationally. This can be achieved through initiatives that improve market infrastructure, provide market information, and enhance the bargaining power of small-scale producers.

For example, partnerships can be formed to develop digital platforms connecting farmers with buyers, providing them with real-time market information and enabling direct sales. Governments can support these initiatives by providing infrastructure, such as internet connectivity and market facilities, and by creating favourable regulatory environments.

Case Study: Fair Trade Partnerships
The Fairtrade Foundation is a PPP that aims to enhance market access for smallholder farmers by promoting fair trade practices. This collaboration involves government agencies, fair trade organizations, and private companies working together to create a fairer and more transparent market environment for farmers.

Through this partnership, farmers receive support in obtaining fair trade certification, which allows them to access premium markets and receive better prices for their products. The partnership also includes initiatives to improve market infrastructure, such as developing farmer cooperatives and establishing fair trade market hubs. These efforts have significantly improved the livelihoods of smallholder farmers, promoting social equity and economic sustainability.

Policy Advocacy and Regulatory Support

Effective policy and regulatory frameworks are essential for the success of sustainable agriculture initiatives. PPPs can play a crucial role in advocating for and shaping policies that support sustainable agricultural practices and create an enabling environment for innovation and investment.

Collaborative Policy Development
PPPs provide a platform for diverse stakeholders to come together and collaborate on policy development. By involving both public and private sector representatives, these partnerships can ensure that policies are well-informed, balanced, and aligned with the needs and realities of the agricultural sector.

For example, PPPs can facilitate multi-stakeholder dialogues and consultations to gather input on policy issues, such as land use, water management, and agricultural subsidies. These consultations can help identify policy gaps and opportunities, leading to the development of more effective and inclusive policies that promote sustainable agriculture.

Capacity Building and Knowledge Transfer
Building the capacity of farmers, agricultural workers, and other stakeholders is essential for the successful implementation of sustainable agriculture practices. PPPs can play a vital role in facilitating capacity building and knowledge transfer through training programs, extension services, and knowledge-sharing platforms.

Training and Extension Services
PPPs can support the development and delivery of training and extension services that equip farmers with the knowledge and skills needed to adopt sustainable practices. These services can cover a wide range of topics, including soil health management, integrated pest management, water conservation, and climate-resilient farming.

For example, partnerships can be formed to develop farmer training programs that combine theoretical knowledge with practical demonstrations. Governments can provide funding and infrastructure for training centers, while private sector partners contribute expertise and resources for curriculum development and delivery.

Conclusion
Public-private partnerships are a powerful tool for driving sustainable growth in agriculture. By leveraging the strengths of both the public and private sectors, these collaborations can address critical challenges, harness innovation, and create an enabling environment for sustainable agriculture. Through initiatives that focus on technology adoption, supply chain sustainability, financing, market access, policy advocacy, and capacity building, PPPs can play a pivotal role in transforming the agricultural sector and promoting a greener, more resilient future.

5.3 Entrepreneurial Strategies for Entering the Sustainable Agriculture Market

The Green Gold Rush
The burgeoning field of sustainable agriculture presents an unprecedented opportunity for entrepreneurs. With the global emphasis on sustainability and increasing consumer demand for eco-friendly products, the market for green agricultural solutions is expanding rapidly. This section provides a detailed roadmap for entrepreneurs looking to enter and thrive in the sustainable agriculture market.

Understanding the Market Landscape
Before diving into the specifics of entrepreneurial strategies, it's crucial to understand the current market landscape. Sustainable agriculture is not just about farming practices; it's about creating a holistic ecosystem that balances economic viability, environmental health, and social equity. This involves everything from organic farming and renewable energy use to fair labour practices and community engagement.

Market Trends and Opportunities
1. Organic Farming: The global organic food market is projected to continue its robust growth, driven by increasing health consciousness among consumers. Entrepreneurs can tap into this market by offering certified organic products.
2. AgriTech Innovations: Technological advancements such as precision farming, IoT, and AI are revolutionizing sustainable agriculture.

Entrepreneurs can develop or invest in technologies that enhance efficiency and sustainability.
3. Renewable Energy Integration: Using renewable energy sources like solar and wind in farming operations can significantly reduce carbon footprints and operational costs. This presents a dual opportunity for entrepreneurs focused on both agriculture and clean energy.
4. Sustainable Supply Chains: Consumers are increasingly demanding transparency and sustainability throughout the supply chain. Entrepreneurs can create value by ensuring their operations adhere to high sustainability standards.

Identifying Your Niche
One of the first steps for any entrepreneur is to identify a niche within the broader sustainable agriculture market. This involves assessing your strengths, resources, and market demand. The following are potential niches to look at:

1. Organic Produce: Focus on growing and selling organic fruits, vegetables, and grains.
2. AgriTech Solutions: Develop software or hardware solutions that improve farming efficiency and sustainability.
3. Renewable Energy Farms: Establish farms that use only renewable energy sources for their operations.
4. Sustainable Livestock Farming: Implement practices that ensure the humane and environmentally friendly raising of animals.
5. Vertical Farming: Use innovative farming techniques to grow crops in urban environments, reducing the need for transportation and land use.

Building a Sustainable Business Model
A sustainable business model is key to long-term success in the sustainable agriculture market. This involves balancing profitability with environmental and social responsibility.

Key Components
1. Value Proposition: Clearly define what makes the product or service unique. Is it the sustainability aspect, the quality, or the innovative technology?
2. Revenue Streams: Identify multiple revenue streams to ensure financial stability. This could include direct sales, subscriptions, and partnerships.
3. Cost Structure: Understand the costs involved in sustainable farming, from initial setup to ongoing maintenance. Look for ways to minimize

costs without compromising on quality.
4. Customer Segments: Identify who the customers are and tailor the marketing strategies accordingly. This could include health-conscious consumers, eco-friendly businesses, and government agencies.
5. Channels: Determine the best channels to reach your customers. This could include online platforms, farmer's markets, and retail partnerships.

Securing Funding and Investment
Securing funding is often one of the biggest challenges for entrepreneurs in any field, and sustainable agriculture is no exception. However, the growing interest in sustainability has opened up numerous funding opportunities:

1. Government Grants: Many governments offer grants and subsidies for sustainable agriculture projects. Research and apply for these opportunities.
2. Impact Investors: Investors focused on social and environmental impact are increasingly looking for opportunities in sustainable agriculture. Pitch the business as a viable and impactful investment.
3. Crowdfunding: Platforms like Kickstarter and GoFundMe can be effective for raising funds and generating public interest in your project.
4. Venture Capital: While traditional venture capitalists may be hesitant, specialized funds focused on sustainability and AgriTech are more likely to invest.
5. Loans: Some banks and financial institutions offer loans specifically for sustainable agriculture projects. These generally need a formal and very solid business plan to secure these loans – probably a last resource (JH).

Implementing Sustainable Practices
To be truly successful in sustainable agriculture, it's essential to implement practices that minimize environmental impact while maximizing productivity and profitability.

Best Practices
1. Soil Health: Use organic fertilizers and crop rotation to maintain healthy soil.
2. Water Conservation: Implement drip irrigation and rainwater harvesting to reduce water usage.
3. Energy Efficiency: Use energy-efficient equipment and renewable energy sources to power your operations.
4. Waste Management: Implement composting and recycling programs to

minimize waste.
5. Biodiversity: Promote biodiversity by planting a variety of crops and maintaining natural habitats around your farm.

Marketing and Branding

Marketing and branding are critical components of any successful business. In the sustainable agriculture market, it's essential to communicate the company commitment to sustainability clearly and effectively.

Marketing Strategies

1. Storytelling: Share the story behind your business and your commitment to sustainability. This can create an emotional connection with your customers.
2. Certifications and Labels: Obtain certifications such as USDA Organic, Fair Trade, and Rainforest Alliance to build trust with consumers.
3. Social Media: Use social media platforms to reach a broader audience and engage with your customers.
4. Partnerships: Partner with other sustainable brands and organizations to amplify your message and reach new customers.
5. Educational Content: Create content that educates consumers about the benefits of sustainable agriculture. This can include blog posts, videos, and workshops.

Building a Resilient Supply Chain

A resilient supply chain is crucial for the long-term success of any agricultural business. This involves building relationships with suppliers, distributors, and retailers who share your commitment to sustainability.

Supply Chain Strategies

- Local Sourcing: Source materials and products locally to reduce transportation costs and support local economies.
- Transparency: Ensure transparency throughout your supply chain by tracking and reporting on sustainability metrics.
- Collaboration: Collaborate with other businesses and organizations to share resources and knowledge.
- Risk Management: Develop a risk management plan to address potential disruptions in your supply chain.
- Continuous Improvement: Continuously assess and improve your supply chain practices to ensure they remain sustainable and resilient.

<u>Navigating Regulatory Challenges</u>
Regulatory challenges are a significant concern for entrepreneurs in the sustainable agriculture market. Understanding and complying with regulations is essential for avoiding legal issues and building a reputable business.

1. Stay Informed: Keep up-to-date with local, national, and international regulations related to sustainable agriculture.
2. Compliance: Ensure your business complies with all relevant regulations, from environmental standards to labour laws.
3. Advocacy: Advocate for policies that support sustainable agriculture and engage with policymakers to influence positive change.
4. Certification: Obtain the necessary certifications to demonstrate your commitment to sustainability and regulatory compliance.
5. Legal Support: Hire legal experts who specialize in agricultural and environmental law to navigate complex regulatory landscapes.

The Way Ahead
The sustainable agriculture market offers immense opportunities for entrepreneurs willing to innovate and commit to sustainable practices. By understanding the market landscape, identifying a niche, building a sustainable business model, securing funding, implementing best practices, marketing effectively, building a resilient supply chain, and navigating regulatory challenges, entrepreneurs can create a thriving business that contributes to a greener, more sustainable future.

The journey may be challenging, but the rewards, both financial and environmental, are well worth the effort. As we move towards a more sustainable world, entrepreneurs in the sustainable agriculture market will play a crucial role in shaping the future and resilience of our food systems.

5.4 Strategic Roadmap for Policy Makers and Entrepreneurs
In this chapter, we have navigated the intricate landscape of sustainable agriculture by outlining a strategic roadmap for policymakers and entrepreneurs.

We began by emphasizing the importance of developing policies that support sustainable agricultural practices. These policies are the bedrock upon which we can build a resilient and eco-friendly agricultural sector.

We also explored the pivotal role of public-private partnerships, highlighting how collaboration between government entities and private enterprises can drive sustainable growth. Such partnerships not only foster innovation but also ensure the efficient allocation of resources and expertise.

For entrepreneurs looking to enter the sustainable agriculture market, we discussed various strategies to carve out a niche in this burgeoning field. From leveraging technology to adopting regenerative practices, entrepreneurial ventures have a plethora of opportunities to make a significant impact.

Lastly, we projected future trends and predictions, underscoring the evolving dynamics of sustainable agriculture and ESG integration. The trajectory suggests a promising alignment of economic viability and environmental stewardship, paving the way for a sustainable future.

Key takeaways include the necessity of robust policy frameworks, the power of collaborative efforts through public-private partnerships, strategic entrepreneurial approaches, and staying abreast of future trends.

As we move forward, both policymakers and entrepreneurs must remain adaptive, innovative, and committed to sustainability principles. These actionable insights will not only contribute to individual success but also to the broader goal of achieving a sustainable agricultural ecosystem.

Overall Conclusions

As we reach the end of 'Green from Green III - Sustainable Harvest: The Intersection of Agriculture and ESG,' it becomes clear that the path to sustainable agriculture is both challenging and rewarding.

Throughout this book, we have explored the evolution of sustainable farming practices, the critical role of Environmental, Social, and Governance (ESG) criteria, and the promising investment opportunities and obstacles faced by stakeholders in the industry.

We've also delved into the innovative technologies that are reshaping agriculture and provided a strategic roadmap for policymakers and entrepreneurs committed to fostering sustainability.

Key takeaways

1. The Evolution of Sustainable Agriculture: Understanding the historical context and current trends is crucial for appreciating the transformative impact of sustainable practices.
2. ESG in Agriculture: ESG criteria offer a robust framework for evaluating and improving the sustainability of agricultural enterprises, leading to long-term benefits for both the environment and society.
3. Investment Opportunities and Challenges: While there are significant opportunities for investment in sustainable agriculture, stakeholders must navigate complex challenges to realize these gains.
4. Innovations and Technologies: Embracing new technologies and innovative approaches is essential for advancing sustainable agricultural practices and ensuring food security.
5. Strategic Roadmap: Policymakers and entrepreneurs must adopt strategic, forward-thinking approaches to promote sustainable agriculture and leverage ESG assets effectively.

Actionable Advice

As you move forward, here is some actionable advice to consider:

- Stay Informed - Continuously educate yourself about the latest trends, technologies, and policies in sustainable agriculture.
- Embrace ESG Principles - Integrate ESG criteria into your business operations to enhance sustainability and attract responsible investments.
- Innovate and Adapt - Be open to adopting new technologies and methods that can improve efficiency and sustainability.
- Collaborate and Network - Engage with other stakeholders in the industry to share knowledge, resources, and best practices.
- Advocate for Policy Change - Work with policymakers to create supportive environments for sustainable agricultural practices.
- By applying these principles and strategies, you can contribute to a more sustainable and prosperous future for agriculture.

Thank you for embarking on this journey with us.

Together, we can cultivate a greener, more sustainable world.

The End

ABOUT THE AUTHOR

Jim Houlihan BEng MSc MBA CEM

Jim Houlihan is a qualified engineer with too many years of experience in offshore oil & gas, mainly in projects and international operations, and held various leadership roles in engineering and project management before moving into renewables, franchising and M&A.

During his more recent journey, Jim has acquired skills and interests that include digital marketing, data analytics, air-to-water and waste-to-energy technologies, hybrid and off-grid power and security solutions, investing in the Energy Transition and latterly, travel photography and writing.

Jim aims to help small and medium companies in developing profitable and sustainable businesses across a range of industries.

Over the years, Jim has lived and worked in Ireland, the UK, across the EU, Brazil, Southeast Asia, and Mozambique and spent a considerable time in the United States.

www.ingramcontent.com/pod-product-compliance
Lightning Source LLC
Chambersburg PA
CBHW050314230526
45471CB00005B/2175